Sicily, Normandy, and
Operation *Market Garden*, 1943–44

COMBAT

US Airborne Soldier

VERSUS

German Soldier

David Campbell

Illustrated by Steve Noon

OSPREY PUBLISHING
Bloomsbury Publishing Plc
PO Box 883, Oxford, OX1 9PL, UK
1385 Broadway, 5th Floor, New York, NY 10018, USA
E-mail: info@ospreypublishing.com
www.ospreypublishing.com

OSPREY is a trademark of Osprey Publishing Ltd

First published in Great Britain in 2018

ISBN: PB 9781472828569; eBook 9781472828552; ePDF 9781472828545; XML 9781472828576

18 19 20 21 22   10 9 8 7 6 5 4 3 2 1

Maps by bounford.com
Index by Rob Munro
Typeset by PDQ Digital Media Solutions, Bungay, UK
Printed in China through World Print Ltd.

Osprey Publishing supports the Woodland Trust, the UK's leading woodland conservation charity. Between 2014 and 2018 our donations are being spent on their Centenary Woods project in the UK.

To find out more about our authors and books visit www.ospreypublishing.com. Here you will find extracts, author interviews, details of forthcoming events and the option to sign up for our newsletter.

Dedication

For Alexander Campbell – Cousin. Actor. Tart.

Acknowledgments

Thanks to the staff at Southsea Library for their inter-library loan work; to the publisher of Greenhill Books, Michael Leventhal, for his kind permission to cite passages from David Isby's work; to Bethan Hoole, assistant librarian at the Hobson Library, Joint Services Command and Staff College (of the Defence Academy of the UK), for making available Major C.N.R. Skeat's 1994 Commandant's Research Paper on the battlegroups in Operation *Market Garden*; to Graham Campbell for logistical support; to Geoff Banks for ruining Paddington; and to Nick Reynolds and the staff at Osprey who turn the raw text into a book.

Artist's note

Readers may care to note that the original paintings from which the color plates in this book were prepared are available for private sale. All reproduction copyright whatsoever is retained by the publishers. All inquiries should be addressed to:

www.steve-noon.co.uk

The publishers regret that they can enter into no correspondence upon this matter.

Comparative ranks

US Army	Heer (Infanterie)	Waffen-SS
General of the Army	*Generalfeldmarschall*	*Reichsführer-SS*
General	*Generaloberst*	*SS-Oberstgruppenführer*
Lieutenant General	*General der Infanterie*	*SS-Obergruppenführer*
Major General	*Generalleutnant*	*SS-Gruppenführer*
Brigadier General	*Generalmajor*	*SS-Brigadeführer*
n/a	n/a	*SS-Oberführer*
Colonel	*Oberst*	*SS-Standartenführer*
Lieutenant Colonel	*Oberstleutnant*	*SS-Obersturmbannführer*
Major	*Major*	*SS-Sturmbannführer*
Captain	*Hauptmann*	*SS-Hauptsturmführer*
1st Lieutenant	*Oberleutnant*	*SS-Obersturmführer*
2nd Lieutenant	*Leutnant*	*SS-Untersturmführer*
Sergeant Major	*Stabsfeldwebel*	*SS-Sturmscharführer*
Master Sergeant	*Oberfeldwebel*	*SS-Hauptscharführer*
Staff Sergeant	*Feldwebel*	*SS-Oberscharführer*
Sergeant	*Unterfeldwebel*	*SS-Scharführer*
Corporal	*Unteroffizier*	*SS-Unterscharführer*
n/a	*Obergefreiter*	*SS-Rottenführer*
Lance Corporal	*Gefreiter*	*SS-Sturmmann*
Private First Class	*Obergrenadier/Oberfüsilier*	*SS-Oberschütze*
Private	*Grenadier/Füsilier*	*SS-Schütze*

Key to military symbols

XXXXX Army Group	XXXX Army	XXX Corps	XX Division	X Brigade	III Regiment	II Battalion
I Company/Battery	••• Platoon	•• Section	• Squad	Infantry	Artillery	Cavalry
Airborne	Unit HQ	Air defence	Air Force	Air mobile	Air transportable	Amphibious
Anti-tank	Armour	Air aviation	Bridging	Engineer	Headquarters	Maintenance
Medical	Missile	Mountain	Navy	Nuclear, biological, chemical	Ordnance	Parachute
Reconnaissance	Signal	Supply	Transport movement	Fortress or static	MG Fortress machine gun	

Key to unit identification

Unit identifier — Parent unit
Commander
(+) with added elements
(–) less elements

CONTENTS

Introduction

The men who made up America's parachute regiments in World War II were some of the best the US Army had to offer; privates in an airborne unit often had the intelligence and initiative that would make them candidates for NCO positions in the regular infantry, their sergeants had to be able to do their own job as well as those of their fellow NCOs and the junior officers that led them, and their officers of all grades had a reputation for hard work and leading from the front – a fact reflected in their casualty figures.

From the outset US paratroop formations justifiably considered themselves an elite, though it would take a little time for their operational capabilities

US paratroopers, likely from Lieutenant Colonel Benjamin Vandervoort's 2d Battalion, 505th Parachute Infantry Regiment (2/505th), stand guard over wounded German soldiers at the Waalbrug road bridge in the Netherlands during Operation *Market Garden*. Though the idea of using parachute troops to make dramatic incursions into enemy territory had been present in most of the major military powers throughout the 1930s, the US decision to develop an airborne capability was (like the British endeavors) essentially reactive. The exploits of German *Fallschirmjäger* during the fall of France and the Low Countries in May–June 1940 showed off their daring tactical utility, while the assault on Crete in May 1941 demonstrated the strategic potential of such forces when employed boldly and on a large scale. (© Hulton-Deutsch Collection/CORBIS/Corbis via Getty Images)

to be fully realized, not least because many in the regular Army were none too enamored of the idea of "elite" units in general, especially ones that were so costly to train, equip, and deploy. Nevertheless, the extremely high quality of the parachute infantry regiments allowed them to compensate for early operational mistakes, and once the lessons of those mistakes had been fully absorbed they provided the Army with a strategic capability that could threaten any part of the Axis front with envelopment from the air.

The Germans had made the running in airborne warfare in the first years of the war, but as the Wehrmacht gradually turned from offensive to defensive operations, it became clear that it would have to find some system for dealing with prospective enemy incursions from the sky. Airborne operations promised great things, but the very boldness of their execution could also be their greatest weakness. Generalfeldmarschall Albert Kesselring thought that

> An air landing, more so than any operation on the ground, is a thrust into unknown territory. The conventional means of reconnaissance and sources of information offer inadequate results and require a great deal of time. From the moment the airborne troops land, they face surprises against which they are not protected by advance reconnaissance and security measures and from which they are no longer able to escape. Consequently, every airborne operation involves a greater risk than ordinary ground combat, requires more time for preparation, and entails a distinct moment of weakness during the first phase of landing. (PAM 20-232 1951: 40–41)

A German soldier relaxes after receiving first aid and a cigarette from a member of a medical unit of the 82d Airborne Division during the first week of the Normandy campaign. The performance of German units in Normandy and the Netherlands was impressive, with many fighting more tenaciously than their composition would suggest, often relying upon their small core of veterans to keep things functioning. The Germans understood that, rather than disband such battle-hardened forces, it was better to let them operate as reduced *Kampfgruppen*, leavened with drafts of replacements to keep the fighting strength up until the time came to withdraw them from the line for a proper rest and full refitting. (Photo12/ UIG/Getty Images)

MAP KEY

The battle for Crete had reframed the idea of what an airborne action could achieve. The Allied airborne efforts grew larger and more daring, from commando-style raids up to battalion and then regimental jumps, the most important of which was that of the 505th Parachute Regimental Combat Team (505th PRCT) over Sicily in 1943. Despite the problems and in some cases outright disasters of that campaign (especially the damage done to the succeeding wave that suffered the loss of many planes shot down by their own side), the paratroopers made a decisive difference to the success of the amphibious landings, confusing the German and Italian defenders, and spoiling their attempts to interfere with the invasion beaches. Sicily proved the value of large airborne operations, as well as the capabilities of the men who had been entrusted with achieving their objectives. The European airborne operations in 1944–45 would all be large-scale strategic endeavors. Operation *Overlord* would be the largest assault to date, dropping three airborne divisions (the 82d, 101st, and British 6th) on Normandy's Cotentin peninsula, followed two months later by the 517th Regimental Combat Team (517th RCT) jumping into southern France as part of Operation *Dragoon*.

The stalling of the Allied push through the Low Countries in late summer 1944 spurred Field Marshal Bernard Montgomery to develop the plan that would become Operation *Market Garden*. Montgomery's proposal was nothing if not bold, arguing for an airborne-led 64-mile incursion across enemy-held territory, with three airborne divisions – the 101st, 82d, and British 1st – securing all the key bridges on the way to the Rhine. If it worked, it would completely bypass all the German Army's prepared defenses, more or less liberating the Netherlands and putting the Allies on the Rhine in less than a week. The speed with which the whole undertaking was orchestrated – seven days from proposal to the drop – was breathtaking, and success would be tantalizingly close, but reconnaissance failures, planning mistakes, and bad luck led to the annihilation of the British 1st Airborne Division at Arnhem. The final airborne effort – Operation *Varsity*, launched toward the end of March 1945 – made good on *Market Garden*'s failings. It was the largest airborne landing in history and would prove to be a complete success, comprehensively breaching the German defense of the Rhine.

1   **July 9–10, 1943:** Operation *Husky* (504th PRCT, 505th PRCT)

2   **September 13–14, 1943:** Operation *Avalanche* (504th PRCT, 505th PRCT, 509th Parachute Infantry Battalion)

3   **June 6, 1944:** Operation *Overlord* (82d Airborne: 505th, 507th, 508th PIRs; 101st Airborne: 501st, 502d, 506th PIRs)

4   **August 15, 1944:** Operation *Dragoon* (517th RCT)

5   **September 17, 1944:** Operation *Market* (82d Airborne: 504th, 505th, 508th PIRs; 101st Airborne: 501st, 502d, 506th PIRs)

6   **March 24, 1945:** Operation *Varsity* (17th Airborne: 507th, 513th PIRs)

The generally shambolic response to the US and British drops in Sicily proved that fending off paratroop and glider attacks was not something that should be left to the proclivities of the local commander; rather it required purpose-built defenses and an evolution in doctrine. Generalfeldmarschall Erwin Rommel, given the role of defending Normandy from any prospective Allied invasion, took the threat posed by air-landed forces very seriously, and developed a number of passive defensive measures designed to cause maximum disruption to the landings of air-dropped and gliderborne troops. In terms of the doctrine that defending units should employ when dealing with paratroopers, Rommel stressed an initial response that was immediate and overwhelming, destroying the attacker before he had a chance to establish himself properly. Such an approach married well with the German practice of forming ad hoc *Kampfgruppen* (combined-arms battlegroups) to deal with specific problems when in combat situations, but it did rely upon the quality of the troops available, their vehicles and firepower, and especially the skill of their commanders.

The Opposing Sides

OPPOSITE Paratroopers, one of whom carries a .45-caliber M1928A1 Thompson SMG, posing in the doorway of a Douglas C-47 Skytrain transport as they load up in preparation for the jump into the Netherlands, September 1944. The M1928A1 (along with its more quickly and cheaply produced successors, the M1 and M1A1) proved to be a popular and versatile weapon, despite its relative weight and complexity, well-suited to the needs of paratroopers. Lieutenant Carl H. Cartledge of the 501st Parachute Infantry Regiment wrote: "The Thompson shoots naturally from the hip and this reveals its great advantage in combat. Shoulder shooters in combat often don't live very long. The best combat carry is high with the muzzle up because the Thompson drops down quicker than it swings up. The second best carry is across the body with the muzzle pointed left. Shots from left to right hit better … because they follow the natural flow of the gun" (quoted in Pegler 2010: 70). (Popperfoto via Getty Images)

ORIGINS AND DOCTRINE

US

Starting on June 25, 1940, US experimentation in airborne warfare led to the founding of the first parachute battalion (the 501st) on October 1, followed by the establishment of the Provisional Parachute Group on February 25, 1941 whose role was to oversee the development of tactical doctrine and associated training literature, as well as to manage the recruitment and training of newly activated units. Further battalion-sized units were activated throughout 1941, with a step-change occurring on January 30, 1942 when four regiments were raised (followed by four more later in 1942 and a further six in 1943), while on March 21 the Provisional Parachute Group evolved into the Airborne Command. Four days later the 82d Division, a famous infantry division from World War I, was reactivated under the command of Major General Omar Bradley at Camp Clairborne in Louisiana.

From June 26, 1942 the 82d Division was under the command of Major General Matthew Ridgway, who oversaw the unit's redesignation as the United States' first airborne division on August 15, 1942. It was comprised of: the 325th and 326th Glider Infantry regiments (GIR); the 504th Parachute Infantry Regiment (PIR); three artillery battalions, the 319th and 320th Glider Field Artillery battalions and the 376th Parachute Field Artillery Battalion (PFAB); the 307th Airborne Engineer Battalion (AEB), made up of two glider companies and one parachute company; and the 307th Airborne Medical Company and other supporting elements. Ground training of the 82d Airborne Division was conducted at Camp Clairborne until October 1, 1942, when the division moved to Fort Bragg, North Carolina, for more advanced ground training in alternation with airborne training. On February 12, 1943 the regimental balance was reversed, with

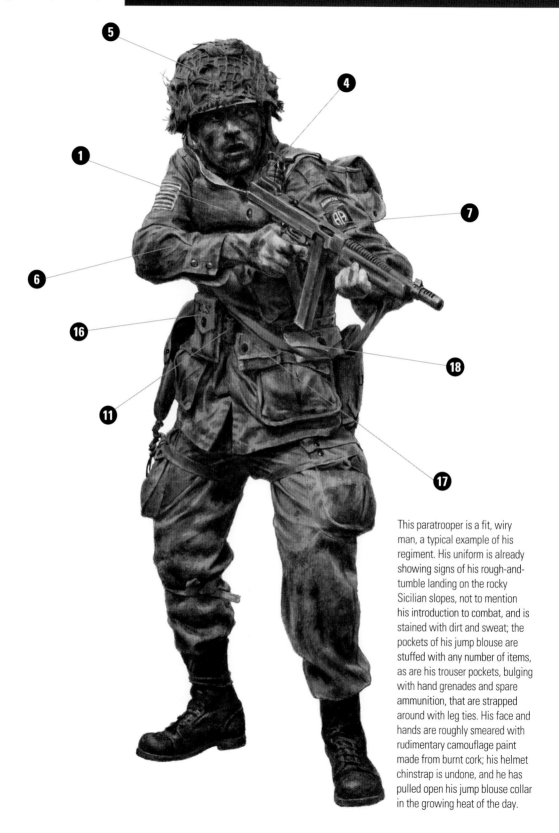

This paratrooper is a fit, wiry man, a typical example of his regiment. His uniform is already showing signs of his rough-and-tumble landing on the rocky Sicilian slopes, not to mention his introduction to combat, and is stained with dirt and sweat; the pockets of his jump blouse are stuffed with any number of items, as are his trouser pockets, bulging with hand grenades and spare ammunition, that are strapped around with leg ties. His face and hands are roughly smeared with rudimentary camouflage paint made from burnt cork; his helmet chinstrap is undone, and he has pulled open his jump blouse collar in the growing heat of the day.

Weapons, dress, and equipment

The paratrooper is armed with a Thompson M1928A1 SMG (**1**) that takes 20-round box magazines, an M1911A1 pistol in an M1916 holster (**2**) on his right hip, an M3 fighting knife in an M6 scabbard (**3**) strapped to the bottom of his right leg, and a pair of Mk II hand grenades (**4**) hooked on to his suspenders.

He wears the M2 helmet (**5**) covered in ¾in netting into which he has woven burlap scrim; his uniform is the M1942 jump blouse (**6**) with the 82d Airborne Division's distinctive "AA" (All American) patch (**7**) on his left shoulder and a roughly made cotton invasion flag (**8**) on his right shoulder, M1942 jump trousers

(**9**) with leg ties, and brown "Corcoran" jump boots (**10**). He wears an M1936 pistol belt (**11**) and M1936 suspenders to support his pack and equipment, which consists of an M1936 haversack (**12**) commonly known as a musette bag, an M1910 "T-handled" entrenching tool (**13**) on his left hip, a five-cell Thompson magazine pouch (**14**) in the small of his back, an M1910 canteen in M1941 cover (**15**), an M1923 pistol magazine pouch (**16**) that carries two spare seven-round magazines, an M1938 lensatic compass pouch (**17**), and an M1942 field dressing pouch (**18**). His weapons and equipment weigh around 28lb.

one glider infantry regiment (326th GIR) replaced by another parachute infantry regiment (505th PIR), as well as the addition of the 456th PFAB. The division sailed from New York on April 29 and landed at Casablanca on the northwest coast of Morocco on May 10, moving first to Oujda in eastern Morocco and then from June 24 into its staging airfields in Tunisia.

Airborne divisions were around 8,400 men strong (some way short of the 15,000-plus men in a "leg" infantry division), in part due to resistance within the higher command toward "special" units, and also because of how they were expected to fight:

> [Chief of Army Ground Forces Lieutenant General Lesley J.] McNair insisted that airborne divisions be kept as small as possible in line with how they would conduct their assaults, secure their objectives, and be quickly relieved to prepare for their next operation. Armament and equipment would be light, with most items being air transportable. Service support assets were kept to the bare minimum, and intended for a short period of intense combat. (Rottman 2006a: 29)

Operation *Husky* would be a cause of some consternation and considerable argument as to the utility of airborne operations, resulting in Training Circular 113 *Employment of Airborne and Troop Carrier Forces*, published in October 1943. The circular was important because while it provided a solid framework for the practical implementation of airborne operations, it also made clear that the responsibility for the use of air-landed assets lay with the theater commander rather than his subordinates. Such an approach ensured that all subsequent operations were undertaken with an understanding that airborne forces would be a strategic asset, the purpose of which was to have a fundamental impact on the campaigns in which they were employed.

German

The history of Panzer-Division *Hermann Göring* stretched back to February 23, 1933 and the foundation of Polizei-Abteilung zbV *Wecke* ("Special Purpose Police Battalion Wecke") in Berlin-Kreuzberg, which had evolved into the Luftwaffe-Regiment *General Göring* by September 1935. Elements of the regiment took part in the takeover of Austria in 1938 and the occupation of Bohemia and Moravia in 1939, followed by the invasion of Poland in 1939 and the attacks on Denmark, Norway, and France in 1940, though it was not until Operation *Barbarossa* in 1941 that the unit as a whole was involved in major combat operations. Pulled out of the Soviet Union in early 1942, the regiment was sent to southern France to refit and undergo expansion, first into a brigade and then into a division. Significant elements of the new formation were sent to Tunisia to help manage the defense against the Allied invasion, an ultimately fruitless endeavor due to the collapse of the Axis in Tunisia. That defeat had a severe impact on the *Hermann Göring* Division, which lost around 10,000 of its most experienced men in one fell swoop. Most of those who fell into captivity had served in the division's prewar incarnations, including a particularly large number of the unit's veteran officers. The rapid attempt to reconstitute the division in the weeks before the invasion of Sicily was necessarily hampered by such a loss, as were the division's command and fighting capabilities.

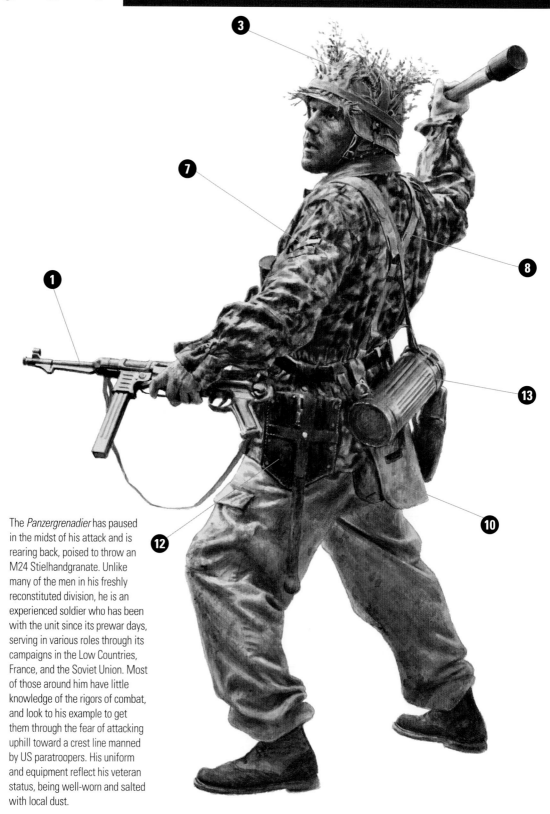

The *Panzergrenadier* has paused in the midst of his attack and is rearing back, poised to throw an M24 Stielhandgranate. Unlike many of the men in his freshly reconstituted division, he is an experienced soldier who has been with the unit since its prewar days, serving in various roles through its campaigns in the Low Countries, France, and the Soviet Union. Most of those around him have little knowledge of the rigors of combat, and look to his example to get them through the fear of attacking uphill toward a crest line manned by US paratroopers. His uniform and equipment reflect his veteran status, being well-worn and salted with local dust.

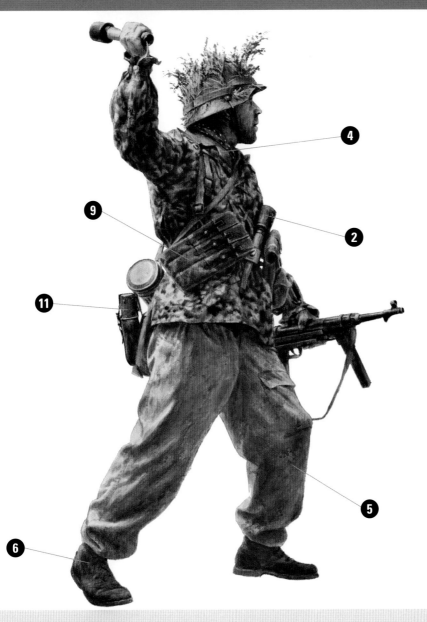

Weapons, dress, and equipment

The *Panzergrenadier* is armed with a 9mm MP 40 submachine gun (**1**) as well as two M24 Stielhandgranate "potato masher" hand grenades (**2**). He wears an M35 helmet (**3**) roughly painted yellow and camouflaged with local flora. His uniform is a tropical variant of the standard M1938 *Feldbluse* and *Langehose* in a lighter material dyed "Khakibraun" (a color closer to tan in reality), and is made up of the *Tropenrock* (tropical tunic; **4**) which was often worn, as in this case, without identifying collar patches, a baggy pair of M1942 *Tropenüberfallhose* (tropical trousers; **5**), easily identifiable by the large map pocket on the left leg, and *Tropenschnürschuhe* (tropical boots with canvas uppers; **6**). He wears the tunic open at the neck, a polka-dot handkerchief tied around his throat to help soak up sweat.

Over his tunic he wears a Waffen-SS M1940 reversible camouflage smock in a "blurred oak leaf" pattern (**7**); his equipment consists of a leather belt and *Koppeltraggestell mit Hilfstrageriemen* (belt supports with auxiliary straps; **8**) on which he carries *Maschinenpistole-Magazintaschen* (**9**) – a matched pair of MP 40 magazine pouches giving him six spare 32-round magazines – as well as an M1931 breadbag (**10**) and an M1931 canteen (**11**), together with a folding entrenching tool (**12**). His gas mask canister (**13**) – the mask itself long-since discarded in favor of a range of personal items – is slung across his back. His weapons and equipment weigh around 38lb.

In June 1944, the US paratroopers featured in this study would fight elements of 91. Luftlande-Division. In Normandy much of the front-line defense was in the hands of *bodenständige* ("static") divisions that lacked vehicles and equipment and which were manned by second-line troops, often with considerable numbers of *Volksdeutsche* (ethnic Germans) from all over Europe in their ranks; the Panzer divisions that made up the strategic counterattacking force against any landings were kept well away from the potential dangers of the coast. As the threat of invasion grew there was a realization that a more immediate reaction to any attack required better units than the *bodenständige*, leading to the reinforcement of the zones behind the beaches with formations such as Fallschirmjäger-Regiment 6 around Carentan and 91. Luftlande-Division northwest of that town. Formed on January 15, 1944 in Wehrkreis (Military District) XII, 91. Luftlande-Division was something of a stopgap formation. At the beginning of June 1944 the 7. Armee report on 91. Luftlande-Division's operational readiness stated that "it was newly organised with three regiments of two battalions each [in reality two *Grenadier-Regimenter* and one *Füsilier-Bataillon*]; weapons and equipment not yet complete; bulk of enlisted personnel young men; training completed only to platoon level; not yet suitable for assault" (quoted in Isby 2004: 67). Oberstleutnant Friedrich-August, Freiherr von der Heydte, commander of Fallschirmjäger-Regiment 6, noted that

> Originally, the 91st Division had probably been designated for combined parachute and airlanding operations – Operation Tanne (fir tree) or Operation Fichte (pine tree), planned for the beginning of March 1944 – in conjunction with the 6th [Fallschirmjäger] Regiment in one of the northern countries, possibly Finland. After this plan was abandoned, the 91st Grenadier Division, like the 6th FS Regiment, was sent to LXXXIV Corps about 1 May 1944. The combat efficiency of this division was poor. (Heydte 1954: 9)

Created on October 26, 1943 by the renaming of 10. SS-Panzergrenadier-Division, 10. SS-Panzer-Division *Frundsberg* had a complement of 19,313 men at the end of that year. By March 1944 it had deployed to the Eastern Front where it fought until the Normandy invasion, whereupon it was transferred to France and thrown into the battles around Caen. Subsequently, the division was heavily engaged in the German retreat until its encirclement in and breakout from the Falaise Gap on August 21, where it now numbered some 3,000 men. It was pulled back into the Netherlands with the rest of SS-Obergruppenführer Wilhelm Bittrich's II. SS-Panzerkorps and stationed around Arnhem to rest and refit. As part of this process the division's commander, SS-Brigadeführer Heinz Harmel, took steps to reorganize his existing forces and equipment into balanced *Kampfgruppen* that could react to any emergency situation that might occur: the key *Kampfgruppe* was built around SS-Panzergrenadier-Regiment 21, the only infantry force the division had left, which was augmented by one battalion from SS-Panzergrenadier-Regiment 19 (from 9. SS-Panzer-Division *Hohenstaufen*); a *Panzerjäger-Kompanie* was pulled together (12 7.5cm PaK 40 guns and four 15cm sIG 33 infantry guns) that drew experienced personnel from other units within the division. Elements of the artillery regiment were attached to SS-Panzer-Regiment 10 *Langemark*, SS-Panzer-Aufklärungs-Abteilung 10

was re-equipped with all the remaining halftracks from SS-Panzergrenadier-Regiment 21 and SS-Panzer-Pionier-Bataillon 10, while the division's flak guns (apart from the 2cm Flakvierlings) were concentrated in SS-FlaK-Abteilung 10.

RECRUITMENT AND MORALE

US

At the outset the reactivated 82d Division was an entirely new formation populated with 16,000 draftees who would undergo their basic training as the divisional structures themselves took shape. Initially determined to be an infantry division, the 82d Division embarked on a 17-week training program aimed at converting raw conscripts into fit fighting men. During and soon after this training process the division underwent three key changes: first, it was designated as an airborne unit and had to split itself in two to provide a formative cadre for the newly founded 101st Airborne Division; second, it had to rid itself of all personnel who, for whatever reason, were unsuited to airborne operations, a process that resulted in thousands of men moving out of the division; and third, it had to integrate the newly transferred 504th PIR (and later the 505th PIR). Such changes, however disruptive, made the 82d Airborne Division into a distinctive formation with a strong spirit and a sense of its own status as an elite force, in no small part due to the influx of the highly trained paratrooper regiments – all volunteers – to the division.

Owing to the nature of the operations that they were expected to undertake, paratroopers needed to be more independently minded, versatile, and aggressive than ordinary infantry. Major General James Gavin, who rose from the command of the 505th PIR to running the 82d Airborne Division and who fought in Sicily, Normandy, and the Netherlands, understood the nature of the fighting that would confront his men. He maintained that although airborne operations were particularly prone to confusion, the key to success lay in careful preparation and the willingness of the men to act with initiative and courage (Gavin 1980: 17).

A high level of coordination was required with Troop Carrier Command, but the initial forays in North Africa, Sicily, and Salerno in Italy left a lot to be desired. Much intensive work went into training flight crews and developing tighter operational practices, but there were some issues that were endemic to airborne endeavors. The divisions were always short of logistical support, a result of their stripped-down Tables of Organization & Equipment (TO&E) and compounded by the difficulty of air-delivering heavy weapons and vehicles to an active battlefield. It was thought that such shortcomings would be mitigated by the very short time that airborne units were expected to be in the line (ideally a matter of days); the reality proved very different, however, with parachute infantry regiments usually engaged far beyond their initial deployment, and in such situations the severe lack of consistent logistical support was a serious problem.

German

German divisions trained their own conscripts in *Feldersatz-Bataillone* (field replacement battalions), whose structure mirrored that of the active-service *Bataillone*, allowing for the easy transfer of reinforcements between the two. Such a system helped to create a bond between the raw recruit and the active-service *Bataillon* he could expect to join, giving him a sense of belonging within his regiment and division.

The men of Panzer-Division *Hermann Göring* were initially all volunteers between the ages of 18 and 25 who met strict ethnic, physical, and moral criteria, but the losses in North Africa combined with the expansion of the force into a Panzer division necessitated a loosening of such rules. Men were drafted into the division from other Luftwaffe formations, and a considerable number of officers and NCOs with tank experience were transferred in from the Army. It is reasonable to assume that because of such a rapid process of expansion and amalgamation the new division was not only inexperienced but lacked the cohesion and unit interoperability that would have come with dedicated training. The Allied invasion cut short any such hopes.

Despite 91. Luftlande-Division's designation as an air-landing unit, there is little evidence that it ever underwent specialist training for such a role, despite being equipped with light artillery and antiaircraft guns. In the months prior to the Normandy landings the division lacked the time and resources to turn itself into an effective fighting force, and the horrendous losses it suffered in the first weeks of the invasion led to its disbandment on August 10, 1944.

The Heer and SS formations in the Netherlands were in almost all cases much-reduced versions of their former selves, but many of them still proved to be effective when battle was joined. The German forces around Nijmegen and Arnhem were comprised of a mixture of veterans, keen but inexperienced youngsters, drafts of older men, and some pressed men from ethnic German backgrounds. When dealing with formations (either freshly created or newly rebuilt) made up of disparate groups of men with variable training, experience, and capabilities, the German Army relied on strong discipline (enforced with draconian punishments including the liberal use of the death penalty) to whip such units into shape and keep them effective when they went into combat.

The will to fight remained strong, despite the obviously dire state of affairs on all fronts. This was in part due to the battle-hardened nature of many units, and also to the realization that the soldiers were now defending the borders of their Fatherland and their own homes and families. One should also not discount the effect of Nazism and its adherents peppered among the ranks and junior officers, especially within Waffen-SS formations, as a reinforcing doctrine that stiffened resolve in the face of daunting odds.

A recruitment poster for Panzer-Division *Hermann Göring* from 1943. The division that was to meet the Allied invasion of Sicily was not ready for the realities of combat that it would confront. By 1943 the Wehrmacht "had developed a defensive doctrine that permitted and, indeed, encouraged, the rapid formation of battlegroups, usually based on experienced, regular fighting units. This meant that even with sub-standard troops (including naval and air force personnel) it was possible to bind together effective fighting units" (Skeat 1994: 12). Such would ideally have been the case with the two *Kampfgruppen* that Panzer-Division *Hermann Göring* launched against the 505th PRCT, but poor training and – more importantly – failures of leadership would cost the German formation dearly in the first few days of the invasion of Sicily. (Galerie Bilderwelt / Hulton Archive via Getty Images)

WEAPONRY, TRAINING, AND TACTICS

US

Within the senior echelons of the airborne forces there was an understanding that the chaos of war, always challenging, would be especially severe for large units dropped (often at night) into unfamiliar terrain and which might well find themselves in serious engagements almost immediately. To overcome – or at least mitigate – some of these factors, significant effort was put into the training of such units at every level as well as careful planning prior to their deployment:

Within the divisional units plans were made in great detail and everyone was oriented in every phase of a coming operation. Each man had not only to know his own job but he also had to have a clear picture of the entire situation. This was necessary as many leaders were sure to become casualties and whoever took over must know perfectly the job he was undertaking. Since limited objectives were always assigned [for] the airborne troops no detail was so small as not to be considered in the plans to take and hold these objectives. The location of each squad, crew served weapon, and command post was picked for the offensive and defensive phases of the action long before take off time. (General Board Report 16 1946: 12)

Such actions required very well-trained and -motivated men. Parachute formations were all-volunteer outfits, paid twice as much as regular infantry and supplied with distinctive uniforms that accentuated their difference from the regular rank and file. The training of the initial battalions had also been far more intensive than was usual, Lieutenant William Yarborough of the 501st Parachute Infantry Battalion believing it to have more in common with special forces such as the Rangers than with that experienced by the regular infantry (LoFaro 2011: 19). Such an ethos reflected the view, still predominant at that time, that the role for parachute infantry would be one of specialist insertions behind enemy lines by relatively small (i.e. company- or battalion-sized) units with discrete tactical objectives. That intense ethos bled through when the parachute infantry battalions were expanded into parachute infantry regiments, giving such units a core of extremely competent soldiers.

FM 31-30 *Tactics and Technique of Air-borne Troops* (the 1942 manual on airborne tactics and techniques) considered that "parachute troops may be considered the spearhead of a vertical envelopment or the advance guard element of air landing troops or other forces. They must seek decisive action immediately upon landing. Success depends largely upon rapid execution of missions assigned to subordinate units" (FM 31-30 1942: 32). Surprise was considered a prerequisite for success, as was the assignment of specific missions with limited objectives. In addition, the specialist nature of such troops meant that they should not be employed on tasks that could be achieved just as well by regular units. The tactical employment of parachute infantry regiments grew from early company- and battalion-sized operations into the 505th PRCT in Sicily and on to the divisional jumps in Normandy and the Netherlands.

Most missions were built around the seizing and holding of key objectives until relieved by ground forces, but they could also include disrupting enemy movements to or from the front line, the capture of airfields or key installations, emergency reinforcement (as at Salerno), diversionary maneuvers, disrupting communications, and intercepting supply lines. Once on the ground it was vital for local commanders to assemble and regain control of their forces as quickly as possible, with speed, surprise, and aggression being the most useful attributes in the early hours of a landing. Generalfeldmarschall Albert Kesselring, who as Oberbefehlshaber Süd (Commander-in-Chief South) was responsible for the Axis defense of Sicily, noted that the shock of such attacks, or even the threat of them, could add considerable impact to an operation:

> The psychological effect of vertical envelopment is considerably greater than that produced by horizontal envelopment. It can affect the enemy command and troops solely by reason of its menace – the uncertainty of when and where an air landing might take place. The consequent effect on the population of the country, either positive or negative as the case may be, should also not be underestimated. (PAM 20-232 1951: 42)

Initial operations in Algeria, Sicily, and Italy highlighted many weaknesses in the US employment of airborne assets, arguably the most important of which was the need to land as close to the drop zones in as concentrated a formation as possible. The overall lack of ground mobility endemic to airborne units meant that any reliance upon vehicles to move to objectives was out of the question. As a direct result pathfinder units were established. Drawn from the ranks of the parachute regiments, pathfinders would jump a short time ahead of the main body and mark the correct drop or landing zone using a PPN-1/PPN-2 "Eureka" transponder to signal the APN-2 "Rebecca" airborne transceiver that was housed in the lead transport plane.

A line of paratroopers jump out of a plane during training exercises above Fort Benning, Georgia, 1943. The process of becoming a paratrooper was neither easy nor particularly safe; five jumps had to be made before a man received his jump wings, and the process was inherently dangerous. Lieutenant James Megellas, who would go on to become one of the 504th PIR's more notable soldiers, underwent jump training in 1943, with his class of 86 suffering many casualties and one fatality; only 27 graduated (Megellas 2003: 15). (The Frank S. Errigo Archive/Getty Images)

Pathfinders also used M227 signal lamps, beacon lights, firepots, smoke grenades, and AL-140 colored signal panels to mark drop zones (Rottman 2006b: 39, 62).

Another problem caused by a lack of mobility was exposed when paratroopers encountered motorized or mechanized opponents. Airborne troops were not able to advance, retreat, or counter-maneuver at the same pace as their more flexible enemies unless they could make use of another unit's logistical capabilities or were part of a combined-arms formation. In addition to their relative lack of mobility, the dearth of heavy weapons available to parachute infantry regiments was an issue, especially when encountering armored formations. The issuing of the M1/M1A1 bazooka rocket launcher was a reasonable stopgap and certainly much better than nothing at all, but it could not make up for the lack of an integral antitank capability. Some efforts were made to mitigate such failings by the adoption of the 57mm M1 antitank gun (informally in Normandy, then as a part of an airborne division's TO&E by the end of 1944), as well as up-gunning the divisional artillery from the 75mm pack howitzer to the 105mm M3 howitzer.

The weather would always play a part, too. The Sicilian drop was compromised by strong winds, while the Normandy operation was hampered

Paratroopers make a mass jump during training in England, c.1944. The Sicilian and Italian campaigns taught the Americans many valuable lessons. James Gavin noted that in ideal conditions, a parachute battalion could be delivered in around two minutes into a 1,000×500yd area, and be ready to fight as little as 20 minutes after landing. He asserted that the optimal drop zone was the objective itself, or as close to it as could possibly be managed; once in place, the paratroopers could set about attacking enemy communications and reconnaissance efforts while rapidly gathering their own intelligence (Gavin 1980: 35–36). (FPG/Hulton Archive/ Getty Images)

by fog, and though the initial deployments in the Netherlands were successful, subsequent waves of reinforcements were delayed significantly by poor weather. Such problems were factored into airborne planning as much as they could be, but it was impossible to eradicate the operational risks posed by the vagaries of nature.

German

The first and most effective defense against airborne attack would have been a strong Luftwaffe, but by 1943 German air power in the Mediterranean had been thoroughly suppressed, a situation that only worsened when the Allied focus shifted to the European Theater of Operations in 1944. In Sicily the German approach to defending against airborne incursions was part and parcel of the general plan to repel a seaborne invasion. Early warning of an attack (in the form of alerts from radio-equipped armored cars positioned in key areas) would initiate a counterattack on enemy beachheads from armored units kept some miles inland; there were no specific countermeasures put in place against air-delivered troops. In the event, the scattering of the 505th PRCT caused considerable confusion, with initial panicked reports flooding into the Axis headquarters stating that several divisions-worth of men had been dropped over almost the entire length and breadth of the island. In hindsight it was clear that, scattered and weak though they were,

the paratroopers had caused a great deal of confusion and disruption to the German understanding of what was happening when it was least needed, and they had also proved to be an unexpectedly tenacious tactical problem that interfered with the main thrust of Panzer-Division *Hermann Göring*'s drive against the beachheads. Future encounters would need to be met with a more deeply thought-through response.

It was understood that the first step was to identify an airborne attack, and then communicate that fact to the higher echelons as soon as possible, ideally by radio as telephone systems proved vulnerable to pre-invasion bombing and sabotage. German staff officers who had been on the receiving end of airborne assaults described how

> As soon as the air landings are an established fact, the next step is to determine where they are concentrated, which of the attacks are being made for the purpose of diversion and deception, and how wide an area is covered. This is extremely difficult, especially at night, and usually considerable time passes before some degree of clarity is possible. Therein lies the defender's greatest weakness. However, it is never advisable to delay countermeasures until this clarity has been obtained. In most cases, the situation will remain obscure until the counterattack is launched. It is all the more important, therefore, that reporting should not be neglected during the fighting; this is a matter of training and indoctrination. (PAM 20-232 1951: 28)

In Normandy the defense against airborne assaults (and air support for naval landings) included the installation of significant antiaircraft resources in the form of III. Flakkorps, which led to the transfer of some 3,500 light and medium antiaircraft guns to positions along the Channel coast (Westermann 2001: 174–75). In addition, Rommel developed a coastal front to repel a naval attack as well as a secondary line farther inland intended to stymie airborne assaults before they could link up with any seaborne attack. This inland line was predicated on occupying the areas' strongpoints with considerable

A Karabiner 98k (Kar 98k), the main German rifle of World War II. Chambered in 7.92×57mm Mauser, the Kar 98k was a bolt-operated rifle that held five rounds in an internal magazine reloaded by stripper clips, and was more or less identical to its World War I predecessor (the Gewehr 98) in operation and effect. By 1939 bolt-action rifles such as the Kar 98k were obsolescent, and though Germany was, like all the other major powers, developing gas-operated self-loading rifles, only the Soviets and the Americans were able to field examples in the early stages of the war. The Wehrmacht would develop a series of prototypes, eventually resulting in a new style of "assault rifle" built around a smaller and more controllable cartridge (8mm *Kurz*), namely the MP 43 and Sturmgewehr 44, that allowed its users to put down a much greater volume of fire than the Kar 98k. Such advances, however, came too late and in too small a number to make much of a difference, and in 1945 the majority of German soldiers still carried the Kar 98k. (NRA Museums, NRAmuseums.com)

A German mortar team with their 8cm schwere Granatwerfer 34 mortar photographed in a Normandy field, early July 1944. German mortar fire was usually accurate and intense (each mortar being capable of firing between 15 and 25 rounds per minute), but this was more a result of the well-trained crews that operated them than due to any intrinsic characteristics of the mortar itself. Weighing around 140lb, the sGrW 34 could be broken down into three loads – barrel, baseplate, and bipod – for ease of transport, and it fired an 8lb high-explosive or smoke shell out to a maximum of 2,625yd. In addition to its three rifle companies, a *Grenadier-Bataillon* fielded a heavy-weapons company that had an allocation of six sGrW 34s, as well as four 12cm Granatwerfer 42 mortars, six medium machine guns, and three light machine guns. (Keystone-France/Gamma-Keystone via Getty Images)

numbers of troops, augmented by passive defensive measures concentrated on those spots that might prove tempting to an Allied invasion planner. Such measures included: the laying of extra minefields, augmented by well-signposted dummy minefields; the studding of open areas with obstacles; and finally, the flooding of large zones behind the beaches to make them impassable.

The measures developed to counter paratrooper attacks were called *Luftlandehindernisse* ("air-landing obstacles"). Colloquially known as *Rommelspargel* ("Rommel's Asparagus"), such defenses consisted of a series of wooden logs 9–13ft in length that were erected in fields that were likely landing sites for gliders; such poles were spaced up to 33yd apart and had tripwires strung from top to top with an explosive (usually a Teller mine or hand grenade) affixed to every third pole, forming a spiderweb of obstacles. Generalleutnant Karl Wilhelm von Schlieben, commanding 709. Infanterie-Division, recalled how they were positioned "in open country exposed to air landings, like meadows, pasture land, etc. There was an abundance of such areas, and the lumber for stakes, the so-called 'Rommel asparagus,' had to be cut first. This was a long, wearisome job" (Schlieben 1954: 14).

In the event, on May 28, little more than a week before the Normandy invasion, Allied airborne reconnaissance discovered concentrations of *Rommelspargel* on some of the 82d Airborne Division's proposed landing sites, forcing a hurried reallocation of drop zones to positions nearer the coast. Such a change of tack effectively neutralized most of the *Rommelspargel*, though it had the unfortunate consequence of dropping many of the paratroopers

Generalfeldmarschall Erwin Rommel inspects Normandy's coastal defense system with a group of German officers, 1944. Rommel took an active role in preparing the Normandy coast for invasion by sea or by air. Generalmajor Rudolf, Freiherr von Gersdorff observed that "Our attitude toward the enemy airborne troops would, according to Rommel, have to be of a defensive nature for the time being, for these would only become a menace when the enemy had succeeded in setting up bridgeheads on the coast. In any case, his opinion was that enemy forces would land in the near-vicinity of the coast, and he had therefore ordered the construction of a land front from three to five kilometers from the coast" (quoted in Isby 2004: 34). Rommel's approach may have underestimated the scope and strategic impact that such troops would have on the invasion, especially if they did not land where he expected them to. (Galerie Bilderwelt/ Getty Images)

into zones that had recently been flooded. Generalleutnant Max Pemsel, 7. Armee's chief of staff, observed that

> Seventh Army always expected that the first enemy airborne attack would be coordinated with the sea attack, and that airborne forces might be landed as far as 20 kilometers [12.5 miles] inland. There were two different views held in reference to flooding endangered air landing areas: a. The rivers should be dammed, the sea let in, and airborne landings at certain places made impossible. b. The landing areas should not be flooded, since by so doing the enemy airborne troops would be protected from counterattack. (Quoted in Isby 2004: 57)

In the event, by late spring 1944 7. Armee had decided on the use of flooding, and it caused the 82d and 101st Airborne divisions serious problems.

By the time of the landings in the Netherlands in September 1944 there was no possibility of employing any of Rommel's measures, forcing the defenders into a more straightforward (and ironically more effective) approach. SS-Sturmbannführer Josef "Sepp" Krafft, who was to play an important role in the German defense at Arnhem, observed that "The only way to draw the tooth of an airborne landing, with an inferior force, is to drive right into it" (Krafft 1944). Krafft's aggressive approach was seen as the only sure way of delivering a killing blow to an airborne incursion in the vital hours before it could coalesce and organize, whereafter it would be much more difficult to defeat. In a similar way the fire of antiaircraft weapons was not just concentrated on planes and gliders, but on paratroopers themselves as soon as they landed because they would be extremely vulnerable, unsupported and without cover. It was recognized that "Speed in carrying out a counterattack against enemy airborne troops is essential, because it is certain that the enemy's fighting strength will be increased continuously by means of additional reinforcements brought in by air. In general, only motorized reserves are successful in arriving in time" (PAM 20-232 1951: 31). The ideal was to destroy airborne forces in detail before they had a chance to link up with their ground elements; once that connection had been made the battle was lost.

The officers and men of 10. SS-Panzer-Division *Frundsberg* had undergone schooling for just such an eventuality. Their commander, Heinz Harmel, noted that 15 months of training to counter an airborne landing in Normandy would pay off in the Netherlands in September 1944; the division's preparations particularly stressed the importance of initiative and decisive action among junior leaders (Kershaw 2004: 41).

COMMAND, CONTROL, AND COMMUNICATIONS

US

The particular demands of airborne assaults required leaders at all levels who understood how to fight effectively using the specific advantages – and disadvantages – that were an inherent part of parachute operations. The 1942 airborne manual made a point of stressing that "Prompt, decisive, and intelligent leadership is of great importance" (FM 31-30 1942: 32); it was clear that officers had to be well motivated and self-sufficient because achieving their own objectives, however modest they might appear, could have a dramatic effect on the overall success or failure of an operation.

The airborne forces tended to attract the more adventurous and dynamic officers, and they found a ready home run by men such as Major General Ridgway, Major General Maxwell Taylor (commander of the 101st Airborne Division), and Colonel (later Brigadier General) James Gavin, who would have a major impact on the whole of the US Army both during and after the war. Gavin in particular proved to have a genuine talent for airborne operations, literally writing the US Army's book on the matter (FM 31-30 *Tactics and Technique of Air-borne Troops*). Still only in his mid-thirties, he was not hidebound or afraid to take on the complexities of airborne doctrine and tactics, and the strength and clarity of his approach won him many admirers, including Ridgway.

Paratroop infantry relied upon SCR (Set, Complete, Radio) systems that were common to the rest of the Army. Units at battalion level and below were equipped with the SCR-300 (the back-mounted "walkie-talkie" with a

A stick of paratroopers in a C-47 Skytrain in 1943. Eleven aircraft were needed to transport one parachute infantry company and its equipment, averaging around 15–16 men per plane. For example, during Operation *Market Garden* aircraft No. 5 transported the following: a platoon leader, a radio operator, a three-man LMG team, an antitank grenadier, an aid man, a messenger, and an eight-man rifle squad. The plane also carried two containers (in the first a light machine gun and spare barrel, shoulder pads, four boxes of machine-gun ammunition, a camouflage net, two ammunition bags with a total of ten antitank grenades, and two blankets; in the second, seven boxes of machine-gun ammunition, 20 rounds of 60mm mortar ammunition, two blankets, and a pair of 2 by 4s) (Verier 2001: 67). (US Air Force/Getty Images)

maximum range of 5 miles) and SCR-536 (the "handie-talkie," with a 1.5-mile range); the artillery had the SCR-609 and SCR-610 (5-mile range). The division command net was comprised of SCR-694 and SCR-284 sets (maximum continuous-wave range 25 miles). Division headquarters had the SCR-300 and SCR-610 for interstaff nets and the SCR-193, SCR-499, and SCR-542 (maximum range 60, 250, and 130 miles respectively) for communication with higher headquarters (General Board Report 16 1946: 8–9).

A US Army Air Force Waco CG-4A glider in 1943. Though the "straight leg" glider infantry regiments lacked the glamor of their parachute-equipped brethren (and were initially forbidden from wearing status symbols such as paratrooper jump boots), they were a vital part of all the major airborne operations in 1944. Though gliders like the CG-4A had the capacity to transport 13 troops, they could carry significant amounts of cargo (up to 4,200lb) and deliver it in a much less dispersed way than was the case with the parachute infantry. (US Air Force/Wikimedia/Public Domain)

A German soldier in Normandy, June 1944. He is either a *Panzerjäger*, or (perhaps more likely) a *Panzergrenadier* from the Panzer-Lehr-Division, whose personnel were known for wearing the *Sturmartillerie*-pattern field blouse and splinter-pattern helmet covers throughout the campaign. He is using a Feldfernsprecher 33 field telephone, probably to communicate with his battalion or regimental headquarters. Each battalion's signal section had six field telephones, the regimental signal section a further 12. (LAPI/Roger Viollet/Getty Images)

German

The German approach to command in the field – *Auftragstaktik* ("mission-oriented tactics") – stressed personal initiative and responsibility, typically in the form of a senior officer setting the objective and then allowing his subordinates to work out for themselves how best to get the job done. To work well it was necessary to have junior officers and NCOs who were intelligent, well-motivated, and well-trained, and ideally who were experienced in combat as well. Such men became harder to find as the war progressed, and constant losses made it increasingly difficult to give nascent leaders enough room to develop the skills and experience necessary for them to become effective in battle. Panzer-Division *Hermann Göring*'s poor showing in Sicily was in no small part due to the grievous loss of the vast majority of its experienced officers and men occasioned by the collapse in Tunisia, as well as the poor quality of those officers that remained:

> The division was commanded by Generalleutnant Paul Conrath, who had served as a junior artillery officer in World War I and as a police officer through the mid-1930s before he entered the Luftwaffe Flak service. Although he saw considerable combat on the Eastern Front in command of Flak-Regiment HG, he had no real experience or training to lead a Panzer division. Regimental

command was even weaker; the division's Panzer regiment was commanded by a former bomber pilot, who had been grounded due to nervous problems. (Zaloga 2013: 22)

Nevertheless, troops who were led by inexperienced officers could still give a good account of themselves, as 91. Luftlande-Division did in Normandy, though such effectiveness usually came at a much higher cost in casualties among all ranks.

The main German field telephone was the Feldfernsprecher 33, which weighed 12lb: "The small switchboard for ten lines (kleiner Klappenschrank zu 10 Leitungen) and the field switchboard for 20 lines (Feldklappenschrank zu 20 Leitungen) were used at battalion and regimental levels respectively" (Rottman 2010: 36). Most German field radios lacked the portability of their US counterparts, but they compensated for this by being extremely well made and reliable. German man-portable radios were designated as *Tornister Funkgerät* ("back-pack radio equipment"), usually abbreviated to "TornFu" followed by a lower-case letter and a number to designate the type or modification of radio in use. Feld Funkgerät ("field radio equipment"; FeldFu) referred to portable and stationary radios, while radio sets mounted in vehicles were simply called *Funkgerät* ("radio equipment"; Fu). The common radio at regimental level and below was the 39lb TornFu *Dora* or improved *Dora 2*; it could be operated on the move (one man carrying the transceiver, another the battery pack) and had a voice range of 4 miles and a Morse range of 9.5 miles.

A pair of German NCOs find temporary respite behind the rear wheels of a StuG III assault gun; they both carry Zeiss 6×30 binoculars, and the man to the left has an M1935 dispatch case as well. As with the US and British armies, the backbone of the German Army was its non-commissioned officer corps. The Germans spent considerable time and resources on ensuring that their NCOs were of a high standard; drawn from long-serving soldiers who had shown merit, their training was consistent and wide-ranging, even during the latter stages of the war when the need for fresh NCOs was pressing. They were usually reliable men with front-line experience whose mix of pastoral care, aggression, and leadership were crucial to the continued effectiveness of the Army. (Nik Cornish at www.stavka.org.uk)

Biazza Ridge

July 11, 1943

BACKGROUND TO BATTLE

Operation *Husky* was to be the first significant operation involving US paratroopers. The plan called for the 505th PRCT to jump behind the Gela beachhead in order to block expected Italian counterattacks on Major General Terry Allen's 1st Infantry Division. Colonel Reuben Tucker's 504th PRCT (the bulk of which was made up of 1/504th and 2/504th) would follow on D+1 or D+2 as the situation allowed, jumping into drop zones under the control of the 505th PRCT. The drop zones were located to the northeast of Gela, a fishing village on the southeast coast of Sicily, and were situated to allow the 505th PRCT to seize key strongpoints on the roads leading to Gela, cutting off the coast from enemy troops positioned in the interior. The amphibious landings were to be carried out by the 3d Infantry Division (Major General Lucian Truscott) around Licata, the 1st Infantry Division (Major General Terry Allen) at Gela, and the 45th Infantry Division (Brigadier General Troy Middleton) around Scoglitti.

Gavin and his men were expecting to fight Italians; they had no idea that two German divisions were stationed on Sicily, even though Ultra decrypts had made that fact available to the most senior members of the Allied high command. Initially staged in the Caltagirone area, Panzer-Division *Hermann Göring*, under the command of Generalmajor Paul Conrath, was the core of Interventionsgruppe Ost ("Eastern Intervention Group"), whose role was to contain and destroy any Allied landings in

Major General Matthew Ridgway (with binoculars), Commanding General, 82d Airborne Division, and staff, overlooking the battlefield near Ribera, Sicily, July 25, 1943. Note the sand/green camouflage scheme on the helmets, only used in the Mediterranean Theater of Operations. Ridgway was an Army man through and through, a professional and highly capable officer that some thought rather priggish, or a "stuffed shirt." Others were more enamored, including Hank Adams, the 504th PIR's regimental S3 (operations officer), who praised Ridgway's patriotism, lack of vanity, and thorough understanding of his men's needs (Blair 1985: 55–60). (USAMHI/Wikimedia/Public Domain)

its sector; it was supported by two Italian Army infantry divisions, the 4th, *Livorno*, and the 54th, *Napoli*. Though reasonably well supplied with tanks, including 17 PzKpfw VI Tigers, the reality was that Conrath's division was still understrength, with nowhere near its full complement of *Panzergrenadiere*, as well as being undertrained. While it would go on to better things, at the outset of the Sicilian campaign Panzer-Division *Hermann Göring* was far from a battle-ready formation, understrength and lacking in experienced – and competent – officers. Generalleutnant Fridolin von Senger und Etterlin, the German Army's liaison officer to the Italian 6th Army, thought it a mistake to give the responsibility of

Fallschirmjäger sitting on an SdKfz 231 *schwerer Panzerspähwagen* ("heavy armored reconnaissance vehicle") in 1943. Since the start of July, Panzer-Division *Hermann Göring* had taken to positioning radio-equipped armored cars at key points along the coast between Gela and Augusta in order to observe the approaches to likely invasion beachheads. Such an early-warning system was eminently sensible considering the very poor quality of the Italian telephone network, as well as the mediocre communications systems that connected the German and Italian staff headquarters. (Heinrich Hoffmann/Mondadori Portfolio via Getty Images)

A German soldier observes the impact of German artillery fire, Sicily, July/August 1943. Aside from Panzer-Division *Hermann Göring*, the main German unit in Sicily was 15. Panzergrenadier-Division, commanded by Generalmajor Eberhardt Rodt. Previously the Division *Sizilien*, on July 6 it was newly renamed in honor of 15. Panzer-Division which had fallen into captivity at the end of the war in North Africa. It had three *Panzergrenadier-Regimenter* (104, 115, and 129), Panzergrenadier-Bataillon *Reggio*, and all the usual divisional artillery and supporting units. It was a capable and well-led division, certainly the better of the two German formations on the island. (ullstein bild/ullstein bild via Getty Images)

defending eastern Sicily to such a unit instead of the more experienced and competent 15. Panzergrenadier-Division.

Generalfeldmarschall Albert Kesselring understood the risks posed by an Allied invasion, and was worried that his Italian allies would lack the speed and aggression that were vital if naval and air landings were to be countered effectively. Kesselring made it plain to his subordinates that, whether or not they received orders to do so, they were to move against the invasion forces as soon as the Allied objective became apparent.

When it came, the invasion brought chaos with it. The initial situation was horribly confused, with conflicting reports of airborne landings coming in from most of southeastern Sicily (some the result of deliberate "dummy paratrooper" drops, many from erroneous real paratrooper drops). Though this came about due to a mixture of poor weather, inadequate flight-crew training, and general inexperience in conducting airborne operations on such a scale, the effect on the defenders was almost as significant as it was on the 505th PRCT. The problems were compounded by dismal communications between the Italian and German commands, both of whom would spend the next few days operating more or less independently of one another. Finally, the troops of Panzer-Division *Hermann Göring*, and many of the men who commanded them, lacked training and experience in antiairborne operations, and were unprepared for what awaited them. Kesselring lamented that in the earliest moments of the invasion crucial time was lost, with errors slowing the progress of Panzer-Division *Hermann Göring* in particular (Kesselring 1954: 196).

After notification of the invasion filtered through, Conrath opted to split his command into two columns that would move in parallel toward the landing beaches east of Gela. The western *Kampfgruppe* (with which Conrath himself would fight) consisted of Panzer-Regiment *Hermann Göring* (Oberst Urban), Panzer-Aufklärungs-Abteilung *Hermann Göring*, Panzer-Artillerie-Regiment *Hermann Göring* (two *schwere Abteilungen*), and Panzer-Pionier-Bataillon *Hermann Göring* (minus one *Kompanie*); it was to jump off from its staging area to the southeast of Niscemi toward the Gela plain and push through to the landing beaches of the 1st Infantry Division. The eastern *Kampfgruppe* consisted of the division's main infantry force, Panzergrenadier-Regiment *Hermann Göring* (a total of around 700 truck-mounted *Panzergrenadiere* split between two *Bataillone*), two *Artillerie-Batterien*, and the 17 Tigers of 2. Kompanie/schwere Panzer-Abteilung 504 (2./sPzAbt 504); it was to jump off from the division's main staging area southeast of Caltagirone and head through Biscari and then on to the Gela–Vittoria coastal road, from where it could hook right or left (into the flanks of the 1st Infantry Division or the 45th Infantry Division) as the situation warranted.

US paratroopers jumping from their C-47 Skytrains over Sicily, July 1943. The 505th Parachute Regimental Combat Team jump proved to be something of a fiasco, with adverse weather coupled with flight-crew inexperience leading to dismal drop patterns: "Of the 226 planes that set out, only one in six jumped its troopers into the DZ, or at least close enough to attack designated targets" (Wolfe 1993: 35). (Keystone/Getty Images)

MAP KEY

1 0830hrs: Having reached the Stazione di Acate, Colonel James Gavin, along with Lieutenant Ben Wechsler's 20-strong platoon of engineers from B/307th AEB, assaults Biazza Ridge. Unaware that they are attacking the left flank of Panzer-Division *Hermann Göring*'s eastern *Kampfgruppe*, the attackers come under heavy fire, with Wechsler severely wounded and the rest of the men pinned down.

2 0915hrs: Major William Hagan and elements of 3/505th start to arrive at Biazza Ridge. Gavin orders an immediate attack on the ridgeline, led by G/505th, which is successful. Strong German counterattacks develop as a result.

3 1500hrs: Significant attacks by *Panzergrenadiere* and Tigers come within 50yd of Gavin's command post, but they are broken up by well-directed naval gunfire and the timely support of a battalion of 155mm M1 howitzers from the 45th Infantry Division, forcing the Germans to retreat.

4 2045hrs: Reinforced by a portion of the regimental HQ Company (Lieutenant Harold Swingler), engineers from B/307th AEB (Lieutenant Jim Rightley), and a company of Sherman tanks, Gavin orders a general attack, securing the ridge and clearing the slopes of Axis troops.

Battlefield environment

Colonel Gavin's 505th PRCT was to jump into three main drop zones – T, S, and Q – that ran from the plains east of Gela on a northeasterly axis toward the town of Niscemi. The paratroopers' key objectives were to block the road south from Niscemi (Objective "X") and seize the junction called Piano Lupo on the Gela–Niscemi/Gela–Vittoria roads (Objective "Y"), a vital intersection guarded by a series of 16 pillboxes that controlled the routes to and from Gela. The reality was nothing like the plan, with paratroopers dropped in a broad southern arc dozens of miles long across valleys, plains, and hills. A little over a mile inland,

situated between the two US amphibious landing zones at Gela and Scoglitti, lay an area of high ground running northeast toward Biscari called Biazza Ridge. The southern portion of the ridge overlooked the shallow valley through which the Acate River flowed down to the coast and the Mediterranean Sea, and was crossed by Route 115 from Gela to Vittoria (with a branch road running north along the length of the ridge toward Biscari), as well as the Gela–Vittoria railroad line which ran more or less parallel to the road. Control of the ridge would allow Axis forces to drive an attack into the flank of the US beachheads at either Gela or Scoglitti.

This photograph was taken during the battle for Gela and shows a column of US soldiers – possibly men from the 1st Infantry Division's 26th Infantry Regiment that had landed at Beach "Yellow," but more likely members of Colonel William Darby's "X" Force which had come ashore immediately in front of Gela at 0315hrs on July 10, and which comprised the 1st and 4th Ranger battalions supported by combat engineers – working their way up a nearby hill to attack an Italian pillbox. The image gives an excellent sense of how the flat terrain of the coastal plain could be easily dominated by the nearby heights, as well as the dense and varied vegetation of trees, scrub, and patchy undergrowth that was a feature of the area in general. The most important elements not shown are the orchards and olive groves that patterned the hillsides and fields of the land that lay between Gela and Scoglitti. (Bob Landry/The LIFE Picture Collection/Getty Images)

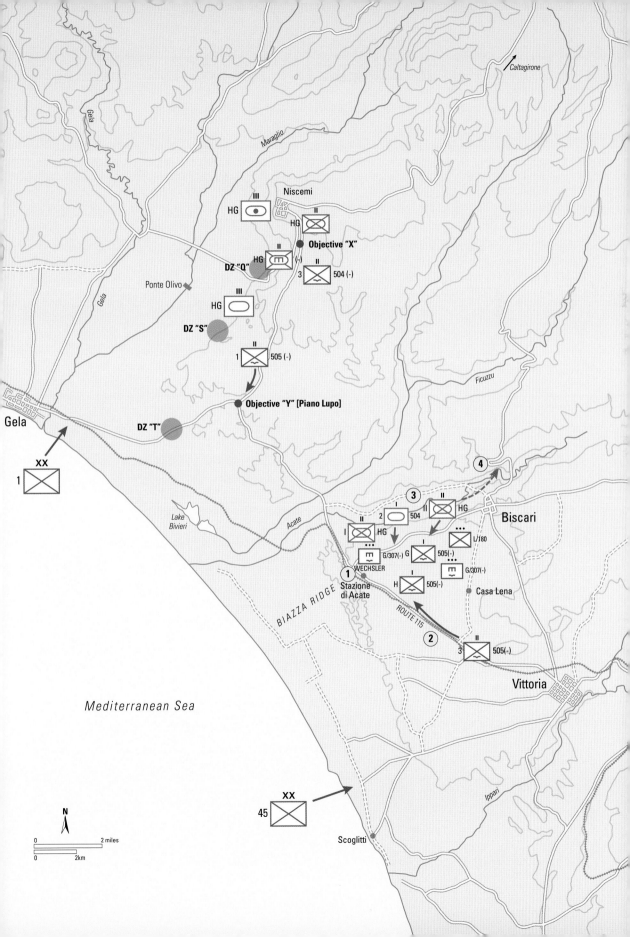

Gela

Mediterranean Sea

Maraglio

Gela

Niscemi

HG III ⦿

HG II

Objective "X"

DZ "Q" HG II (-)

3 504 (-) II

Ponte Olivo

HG III

DZ "S"

1 505 (-) II

Objective "Y" [Piano Lupo]

DZ "T"

XX 1

Lake Bivieri

Acate

Caltagirone

Ficuzzu

4

3

2 504 III

I HG II

II HG

WECHSLER G/307(-) G

1 Stazione di Acate

BIAZZA RIDGE

ROUTE 115

2

3 505 (-) II

Biscari

I L/180 505 (-)

G/307(-)

H 505(-) I

Casa Lena

Vittoria

XX 45

Scoglitti

Ipari

N

0   2 miles
0   2km

INTO COMBAT

Of the 3,045 men in Gavin's force, I/505th was the only unit dropped on target. Seeking out their objectives as well as fellow paratroopers, the men of the 505th PRCT gradually coalesced into two main fighting groups: one, commanded by Lieutenant Colonel Gorham, was made up of around 100 men who had landed near the original drop zones (and would seize the key objectives there); the other, commanded by Gavin, would eventually comprise around 300 men who had dropped quite a bit farther to the southeast around Biscari and Vittoria. After the initial confusion of the landing, Gavin had managed to pull together a small band of around a half-dozen men that included Major Benjamin Vandervoort and Captain Al Ireland, and moved off in search of his objective. His small force became involved in several skirmishes with Italian troops. His group, armed with two carbines (both of which had jammed), a Thompson SMG, an M1 Garand rifle, and a Colt M1911 pistol between them, was in no state to engage in a serious set-to, especially with any sort of enemy armor. Gavin, bitterly disappointed at his first day in combat, sought out a patch of rough, high ground that would be difficult for tanks to approach where he and his men could lie low and rest until darkness.

Despite the potentially disastrous scattering of the 505th PRCT, the mission was clear and most of the paratroopers, after forming into bands of various sizes, attempted to move toward where they thought their objectives were. The experience of a small group of paratroopers (a mix of men from B/307th AEB and A/505th) was typical. Dropped around 15 miles northeast of their objective, the ad hoc battlegroup spent most of the night searching for their drop zone and cutting telegraph wires whenever they came across them, then digging in at a road intersection just before dawn. Their combat diary records how

The reinforced 505th PRCT totaled 3,405 soldiers; it would require 227 C-47s for transport in five groups from the 52d Troop Carrier Wing. Commanded by Colonel James "Jumpin' Jim" Gavin, the 505th PRCT's major elements were: the three battalions of the 505th Parachute Infantry Regiment (1/505th, commanded by Lieutenant Colonel Arthur Gorham, 2/505th, led by Major Mark Alexander, and 3/505th, under Major Edward Krause); the 3d Battalion, 504th Parachute Infantry Regiment (3/504th), led by Lieutenant Colonel Charles Kouns; the 456th Parachute Field Artillery Battalion (Lieutenant Colonel Harrison Harden); and Company B, 307th Airborne Engineer Battalion (B/307th AEB), under Captain William Johnson. Gavin's command also included detachments from the 82d Airborne Signal Company (Lieutenant Edward Kacyainski) and the 307th Airborne Medical Company (Staff Sergeant Kenneth Knott) and US Navy support liaison units. (Bettmann/Getty Images)

Smoke rising from fields outside Gela during an engagement between US troops of the "Big Red One" (1st Infantry Division) with antitank guns (aided by naval bombardment), and German armored forces fighting for control of the town and surrounding area, likely July 10–11. Generalfeldmarschall Albert Kesselring was impressed by the airborne force's contribution: "the parachutists were scattered over a wide and deep area by the strong wind. Operating as nuisance teams, they considerably impeded the advance of the Hermann Goering Panzer Division and helped to prevent it from attacking the enemy promptly after the landings at Gela and elsewhere. This opposition would not have made itself felt so strongly if General Conrath had not organized his troops in march groups contrary to correct panzer tactics" (PAM 20-232 1951: 25). (Bob Landry/The LIFE Picture Collection/Getty Images)

At 0530, a German motorcycle containing 3 passengers pulled up to the crossroads and stopped. The passengers were killed. Another motorcycle arrived 15 minutes later and [was] likewise caught under fire and the occupants killed. The men were then assembled and moved out in the general direction of the DZ. Five of this group were separated when they went to pick up two equipment chutes which were spotted a half mile away. The remainder continued on and took up a position on ground commanding the two valleys. Here contact was made with elements of Company "G," and defensive positions were set up. During the afternoon, 2d Battalion, 180th Infantry, 45th Division, arrived at the hill. The men attached themselves to it and remained with it for three nights and two days. During this period of time additional parachutist[s] drifted in and became part of their organization. (Quoted in 82d Airborne Division 1945: 10)

As for the Germans, word of the invasion reached Conrath not through his Italian allies, but from Kesselring, who radioed Panzer-Division *Hermann Göring* with orders to be formed up and ready to move against the Allied seaborne invaders by midnight at the latest (Kesselring 1954: 196). The eastern *Kampfgruppe* had moved out from its staging area around Caltagirone, its force of Tigers in the vanguard. After the *Kampfgruppe*'s commander had been relieved for stopping every time his column was attacked by random bands of paratroopers, the first day was not without some success, but the force quickly fell back in the face of the 45th Infantry Division. The western *Kampfgruppe* fared no better, finding their way blocked by Lieutenant Colonel Gorham's force around Piano Lupo. Having withdrawn to the staging areas around Niscemi, Conrath received a visit from Generalleutnant Senger und Etterlin who gave him a clear order to do tomorrow what he had failed to achieve today. During the early hours of July 11, both of Conrath's *Kampfgruppen* were to move southwest, with Gela and the surrounding area as their objective (Kurowski 1995: 155).

Benjamin Vandervoort

Benjamin Hayes Vandervoort was born March 3, 1917 in Gasport, New York. Commissioned in 1938, he joined the US Army's nascent paratroop force in the summer of 1940, becoming the parachute training officer at Airborne Command. Promoted captain in August 1942, he was given command of F/505th as the new unit was being formed. Vandervoort was the 505th PRCT's S3 (operations officer) during the Sicily jump and his consistent performance there resulted in his being given command of 2/505th a few months later in October. He was promoted lieutenant colonel on June 1, 1944, and his battalion would form the lead serial of the airdrop over Normandy, dropping on DZ "O" where he broke his leg. Tying the laces of his boot tight and using a rifle as a crutch, Vandervoort took part in 2/505th's battles around Sainte-Mère-Église. Later that year he would lead 2/505th through Nijmegen to secure the southern bridgeheads over the Waal, before he was severely wounded during the Ardennes offensive (he was hit by mortar shrapnel in the face, costing him his left eye), ending his part in the war.

During the early hours of July 11, Gavin's small group met up with elements of the 45th Infantry Division, allowing him to finally find out where he was (a few miles south of Vittoria). Sequestering a jeep, Gavin raced along Route 115 westward with Major Vandervoort and Captain Ireland, when he came across Major Krause and around 200 men of 3/505th. Gavin was none too pleased to find a significant part of one of his battalions sitting in a tomato field when there was fighting to be done, and he ordered Krause to get his men up and moving along the road toward Gela. Shortly after leaving Krause, Gavin ran into another small force made up of a platoon from L/180th Infantry who had wandered into the area, as well as 20 engineers of B/307th AEB under Lieutenant Ben Wechsler, who informed him that the enemy were holding the high ground about a mile farther on down the road.

With Wechsler and his engineers in tow, Gavin continued on down the road to Gela on foot. By 0830hrs his reconnaissance had brought him to the point where the railroad line crossed the Gela–Vittoria road, from where he could see a ridge roughly a half-mile away (Gavin 1978: 29). The tactical value of the 100ft-high ridge, overlooking the main coastal road and railroad line, as well as being between the exposed flanks of the 1st and 45th Infantry divisions, was obvious. Gavin sent Major Vandervoort back to order Major Krause and 3/505th forward, and then to go on to inform the 1st Infantry and 82d Airborne divisions of his plan to establish a defensive line on Biazza Ridge and move toward Gela. In the meantime, Gavin ordered Wechsler and his 20 engineers to advance on the ridge and take it. The initial assault went well enough, but soon small-arms fire increased, wounding Wechsler and pinning down the engineers. The small force had bumped up against the left flank of the Panzergrenadier-Regiment *Hermann Göring Kampfgruppe* as it advanced toward the Gela–Vittoria road.

At 0915hrs 3/505th, about 200 men strong, started arriving under the command of the battalion's executive officer, Major William Hagan, Krause having departed for the 45th Infantry Division's command post to provide a situation update. The platoon of 40 men from L/180th Infantry were promptly dragooned by Gavin and positioned on the right flank. The paratroopers, led by G/505th, were immediately put to work storming up the ridge, where they relieved the pinned-down engineers and pushed on, seizing the crest line and much of the reverse slope. Pouring artillery and

Paul Conrath

Paul Conrath was born November 22, 1896 in Rudow, near Berlin. Upon the outbreak of World War I he joined the artillery, rising to the rank of *Leutnant*. After the war he joined the police service in Berlin, becoming *Adjutant der Staatspolizei Inspektion* ("Adjutant of State Police Inspection") in 1933. During this time he came into Göring's orbit, becoming his adjutant. In 1936 he transferred as a *Major* to Luftwaffe-Regiment *General Göring*, commanding a light antiaircraft battalion and by 1940 the regiment. He would remain the unit's commander through its evolutions up to an armored division, leaving in April 1944 to become *Inspekteur der Fallschirmtruppe* ("Inspector of Parachute Troops") and *Kommandierenden General der Ausbildungs- und Ersatztruppen* ("Commanding General of Training and Replacement Troops") of 1. Fallschirm-Armee. His background as an artilleryman and police officer did not prepare him for the command of a Panzer division, resulting in criticism by Kesselring for his failure to use tried-and-tested armored tactics in Sicily. Nevertheless, his personal bravery (not to mention his good relationship with Göring) saw him promoted to *Generalleutnant* and retain command of his division, adding Oak Leaves to his Knight's Cross.

mortar fire on to the ridge, the Germans quickly counterattacked, forcing the paratroopers back over the crest until timely reinforcement arrived in the shape of H/505th, witnessed by G/505th. The paratroopers pushed the *Panzergrenadiere* down into the valley, but the Germans regrouped quickly for another attack, this time supported by their attached armor, the Tigers of 2./sPzAbt 504.

The fighting was intense in places, but not consistent, with no concerted attempt by the German force to concentrate their efforts and drive hard through a specific section of the ridge; nor was there any attempt at an envelopment, something that their numbers, mobility, and firepower would certainly have allowed them to try. Gavin was sure that his position could have been flanked easily enough – he lacked the men and guns to stop it, especially on his right – but the pressure continued to build up along his main line. The apparent German inability to press home their attacks was noticed by the Americans, who ascribed it to poor commanders or a defensive mindset (D'Este 1989: 293).

The growing intensity of barrages from artillery and 12cm mortars made life uncomfortable for the defenders, especially the use of white phosphorus shells, but the appearance of massive and intimidating Tiger tanks as part of the succeeding German counterattack was a real shock for the H/505th men who had pursued their foes down the western slope of the ridge. The tanks ground their way slowly through the difficult terrain, picking off targets wherever they could find them, then retreating back to their ammunition carriers when they needed to resupply.

The strength of the second German counterattack forced Gavin to pull his men back to the reverse slope of the ridge, keeping them out of the direct line of sight of the Tigers. It would likely have been considerably worse if the *Panzergrenadiere* had worked effectively with their armor, but the *Hermann Göring* troops lacked the training and experience to perform well in a combined-arms assault.

Gavin found there were not enough men to provide anything like a proper defensive line, a weakness compounded by the severe lack of heavy weapons, especially artillery: "Because of the loss of equipment during the drop there were few rocket launchers present. By noon one 75mm howitzer had arrived,

about an hour later another arrived and by the end of the day there were three present" (82d Airborne Division 1945: 26). As for reinforcements, Gavin had to make do with whatever he had to hand, feeding the small groups of arriving paratroopers piecemeal into his overstretched position. Setting up his 75mm howitzers at either end of the ridge, Gavin ordered them to remain concealed and aim for the undersides of the Tigers as they crested the rise (Gavin 1978: 30).

In the early afternoon one of the Tigers began to appear from behind a stone house, moving very slowly, about 400yd away from the main US position. One 75mm crew dragged their howitzer up the ridge until they were positioned in the open, and were promptly bowled over by the shattering impact of an 8.8cm round that detonated just to the front of their gun. After thinking better of retreating, the crew scrambled back to their 75mm piece and engaged the Panzer in a gunnery duel, eventually scoring some hits. Other encounters were less successful, with many bazooka crews finding that not only were their weapons unable to penetrate the German armor, but that the backblast of smoke from the firing of the bazooka's rocket often gave their positions away. The Panzers would use their machine guns and even their main armament in response, as well as driving over the bazooka teams' positions in attempts to run them down; indeed in the aftermath of the battle several dead paratroopers were recovered, their bazookas crushed into their bodies by Panzer tracks.

As the afternoon wore on, pressure on the paratroopers' threadbare battered position was growing once more, but Gavin told his men they would be staying on the ridge (Breuer 1997: 130). Another large counterattack – the third of the day – was developing, when Gavin was greeted by the happy sight of Captain Ireland, who had gone back to the 45th Infantry Division to get help and now returned with gunnery liaison officers from the US Navy as well as from a battalion of 155mm M1 howitzers from the 45th Infantry Division. Gavin observed that "They did splendid work and at about three o'clock were firing upon known German assembly areas and positions. The 45th Division

A PzKpfw VI Tiger tank in a Sicilian village, August 2, 1943. Just prior to the invasion, 2./sPzAbt 504 (comprising 17 Tigers) had been assigned to Panzergrenadier-Regiment *Hermann Göring*. It was not a happy fit, with the unit suffering from poor logistical and mechanical support from the outset. Major Gierga, the commander of Panzer-Abteilung 215, reported that several Tigers became bogged down, while others were cut off and could not be recovered; by July 20 only four remained operational, with a single Tiger surviving to reach the Italian mainland (Jentz 1996: 107). (ullstein bild via Getty Images)

also sent up two 57mm antitank guns. By this time all of the launchers except three had been destroyed and the tanks were within 50 yards of the Combat Team Command Post" (82d Airborne Division 1945: 26).

The thunderous battering they received from the artillery broke the German attack, forcing them back to regroup around 1,100yd back from the ridge. The Germans were well and truly on the back foot, and Gavin decided to make the most of the opportunity, resolving to destroy the enemy force and attend to the American casualties (Gavin 1978: 33). The attack would be augmented by newly arrived reinforcements: a force from the Regimental Headquarters Company, commanded by Lieutenant Harold Swingler; a group of engineers from B/307th AEB, led by Lieutenant Jim Rightley; and lastly a company of Sherman tanks (either six or 11 in number – sources differ). Launched at 2045hrs, the American attack was conducted by every man available; in the teeth of savage artillery, mortar, and small-arms fire it overran the German positions and chased the enemy from the field (Gavin 1978: 33–34). During the advance Swingler came upon the crew of a Tiger outside their tank, in casual discussion; he promptly killed them all with a well-thrown grenade, and captured their tank intact – a first for the 82d Airborne Division.

The *Hermann Göring* situation report for the day, made by Oberst Hellmut Bergengruen, one of the division's staff officers, at 1600hrs, July 11, was pessimistic even before Gavin's last attack, especially considering the actual balance of forces the division's *Kampfgruppen* were facing in their fight to get to the beachheads. It stated baldly that the Axis counterattack had failed, and that the Italians were now to be considered unreliable; in the face of steady Allied reinforcement, remaining in place would entail the destruction of Conrath's division. Instead, German forces should consolidate their defenses in more favorable terrain (D'Este 1989: 295–96). Gavin's resistance had broken the eastern *Kampfgruppe*, with the western *Kampfgruppe* under Conrath faring little better. As both forces fell back on Niscemi Generalleutnant Senger und Etterlin, realizing that Panzer-Division *Hermann Göring* and its Italian allies were not going to reach the beachheads, let alone seize them, ordered a withdrawal to Caltagirone.

La Fière

June 6–7, 1944

BACKGROUND TO BATTLE

The German plans to counter an invasion in Normandy were considerable, but deep flaws would be exposed when the hammer fell. The defense was layered: there were coastal garrisons and emplacements, with rear areas protected by antiairborne measures (*Rommelspargel*, flooding, minefields), and behind them strategic reserves that could reinforce any areas under attack. Rommel wanted to position the reserves near the coast so they could be deployed immediately. Despite Rommel's wishes the heart of the reserves – the Panzer divisions – were kept well back from the invasion zone, and required the specific authorization of the Führer to allow their release. Rommel adapted his plan to strengthen the rear areas behind the beaches by stationing rapid-reaction forces within them, in an attempt to ensure that any incursion by sea or air could be repelled at once. Unfortunately, there were not enough troops available to allow comprehensive coverage of all such areas, and those that he was able to secure were a mixed bag. Generalleutnant Wilhelm Falley's 91. Luftlande-Division was one such formation; it had only been raised at the start of the year, and had been organized and equipped on the basis that it was to be used in air-landing operations. Such adventures never came to pass and the division found itself in Normandy, short of transport, undertrained, and understrength.

The divisional headquarters of 91. Luftlande-Division was at Saint-Sauveur-le-Vicomte, about 9 miles west of Sainte-Mère-Église as the crow flies. It had two *Grenadier-Regimenter*: 1057 (Oberst Sylvester von Saldern, positioned

A German soldier wearing his splinter-pattern-camouflage Zeltbahn 31 shelter-quarter as a simple smock writes a letter, a pile of M24 Stielhandgranaten by his side. By the time of the Normandy invasion the field uniform of the average German soldier was the M1942 or M1943 field tunic, sometimes covered with either a shelter-quarter or a smock (such as the M1943 marsh-pattern hooded smock). Helmets were often camouflaged with specially made covers in a variety of designs, or more straightforwardly with netting, bread-bag straps, or a chicken-wire "basket", used to hold foliage in place. (Nik Cornish at www.stavka.org.uk)

on the road a little over a mile west of Saint-Sauveur-le-Vicomte) and 1058 (Oberst Kurt Beigang, positioned at Saint-Cyr, 2 miles east of Montebourg). Each had three *Grenadier-Bataillone*, one *Infanteriegeschütz-Kompanie*, and one *Panzerjäger-Kompanie*. The division also included Füsilier-Bataillon 191 (made up of three independent units: Fahrräd-Kompanie 191, Panzerjäger-Kompanie 191, and FlaK-Kompanie 191), Gebirgs-Artillerie-Regiment 191 (24 10.5cm GebH 40 mountain howitzers and 12 8.8cm PaK 43 antitank guns), and Pionier-Bataillon 191. The division was still equipped with the weapons that had been assigned to it because of its air-landing role; for

A last-minute check of equipment is made just before this stick of paratroopers board their plane for France, June 5, 1944 (the exact unit is difficult to identify because the censor has obliterated the shoulder patches and helmet markings). The men wear the T-5 troop main harness and parachute with the T-5 troop reserve parachute, and B-4 pneumatic life vest; the average rifleman would be carrying his M2 helmet, an M1 Garand rifle and M1942 bayonet as well as 16 eight-round clips, an M1911A1 pistol with two spare seven-round magazines, a No. 75 "Hawkins" antitank grenade-mine, a No. 82 "Gammon" bomb (a type of grenade), four Mk IIA1 fragmentation grenades, and an M16 orange smoke grenade. He would also have his M1936 Musette bag, an ammunition bag, a first-aid pack, canteen, entrenching tool, TL-122B flashlight, M3 trench knife, a gas mask, a 33ft rope, and any number of other sundry items, both allotted and personal. (PhotoQuest/Getty Images)

example, two of its three *Artillerie-Abteilungen* manned GebH 40 pieces and FlaK-Kompanie 191 used the Gebirgsflak 38, the lightweight version of the 2cm FlaK 38 antiaircraft gun designed for mountain and airborne troops. The GebH 40 was an excellent gun, but its ammunition was not interchangeable with that of the standard 10.5cm leFH 18 light field howitzer; the division only had one basic load of ammunition when it arrived in Normandy, and further supplies were not readily available (Zetterling 2000: 239).

In an attempt to sharpen the division's fighting edge, Fallschirmjäger-Regiment 6 (Major Dr. Friedrich-August, Freiherr von der Heydte) was subordinated to it when it moved into the area at the end of May, stationed around Carentan. A small Panzer force, Panzer-Ersatz- und Ausbildungs-Abteilung 100 (Major Bardenschlager), was also attached to the division; primarily tasked with training new tank crews in the basics of armored maneuver and warfare, it was equipped with obsolescent vehicles, most of which had been captured during the Battle of France. Bardenschlager's command had around 25 tanks split between two *Kompanien*, the majority being Renault R 35s or Hotchkiss H 39s, with a sole PzKpfw III.

Partly through planning, partly through good fortune, the Allied airborne assault would land where it could do most damage to the Normandy defenses – right between the beachheads and the quick-reaction forces that were meant to keep them away from the shore. The 82d Airborne Division's drop was codenamed *Boston*. Lieutenant Colonel William Ekman's 505th Parachute Infantry Regiment would land in three large fields around 1.25 miles to the northwest of Sainte-Mère-Église: 1/505th (Major Frederick Kellam) was to secure two crucial crossings over the Merderet River at Chef-du-Pont and La Fière; 2/505th (Lieutenant Colonel Ben Vandervoort) would move north of Sainte-Mère-Église to block the

A paratrooper of the 101st Airborne Division sits awaiting take-off on the eve of D-Day, holding General Dwight D. Eisenhower's message of good luck in one hand and his M1A1 bazooka in the other. The glider regiments had a battery of eight 37mm M3 antitank guns (unofficially upgraded to the US version of the British 6-pounder, the 57mm M1, by D-Day), but in the first hours of an attack the parachute infantry regiments could only rely on the 2.36in M1 or M1A1 bazookas they brought with them, each battalion having 21. (Photoquest via Getty Images)

Cherbourg road; and 3/505th (Lieutenant Colonel Edward Krause) would take the important crossroads town of Sainte-Mère-Église itself. Lieutenant Colonel George Millett's 507th Parachute Infantry Regiment would seize the western end of the La Fière causeway at the village of Cauquigny, and Lieutenant Colonel Roy Lindquist's 508th Parachute Infantry Regiment would secure crossings over the Douve River at the southwestern edge of the drop zone.

By 0111hrs the first reports of airborne landings had filtered through to General der Artillerie Erich Marcks at LXXXIV. Armeekorps headquarters, causing consternation. There was no way to tell the scale or seriousness of the attack based on those initial reports, but Rommel's plan was clear – the reaction must be immediate, and devastating.

German infantry fighting in Normandy during the first days of the invasion. Despite the presence of units such as Fallschirmjäger-Regiment 6, many of the troops that would bear the brunt of the initial Allied attack were not first-line formations, instead being known as *bodenständige* ("static") divisions that were meant for coastal defense. Generalleutnant Max Pemsel, 7. Armee's chief of staff, noted that "Only a few of the units of these divisions had any transport whatsoever, and their artillery was only partially mobile … as a result of the repeated combing out of replacements for the Eastern front, there was eventually not a man left fit for duty in the East" (quoted in Isby 2004: 58–59). (ullstein bild/ullstein bild via Getty Images)

1 *c.*0115hrs, June 6: 1/505th makes an excellent landing at DZ "O" to the northwest of Sainte-Mère-Église. After gathering his men Lieutenant John Dolan, commanding A/505th, sets out toward his objective, the La Fière bridge over the Merderet River.

2 *c.*1000hrs, June 6: The approach of A/505th is hampered by fire from a platoon-strength body of troops dug in around the bridge and occupying the Manoir. Resistance is gradually overcome, with the German defenders either pulling out or surrendering. By 1430hrs both the Manoir and bridge are firmly in US hands.

3 1600hrs, June 6: A *Kampfgruppe* consisting of troops from Grenadier-Regiment 1057 and tanks from Panzer-Ersatz-und Ausbildungs-Abteilung 100 sets out from Cauquigny in an attempt to break through the US defenses at La Fière. The German attack is repulsed with the loss of three tanks and an undetermined number of infantry.

4 1000hrs, June 7: The *Kampfgruppe* makes another attempt on the bridge, with an attack by four tanks and a large body of infantry supported by heavy artillery fire from mortars and 8.8cm guns. Two German tanks are destroyed (forcing the others to withdraw), but the German infantry press forward, eventually acknowledging defeat by the slimmest of margins.

Battlefield environment

The opening of the locks at Carentan had waterlogged many of the surrounding fields, as well as swelling the Merderet River to several times its usual size, making much ground impassable for both attacker and defender; at La Fière the flooded zone was at least 1,100yd wide according to Lieutenant John Dolan. During the summer months the Merderet is usually little more than a shallow stream, crossed by the La Fière and Chef-du-Pont bridges. Both bridges were relatively small affairs (like glorified culverts), but the roads that crossed them to the west were raised causeways because the fields were prone to flooding during periods of heavy rain. Such an environment was perfectly suited to defensive tactics, caused logistical difficulties (for both attackers and defenders), and also hampered the initial forming-up of some of the parachute units that dropped into them (2/502d, for example, landed on the outer edge of drop zone "C" in dense *bocage* and spent the majority of D-Day trying to assemble rather than fight). Such features would prove to be both a hindrance and a help for A/505th on its way to La Fière, as well as in its defense.

An aerial photograph showing the *bocage* country of the Cotentin peninsula in 1944 prior to the Normandy invasion. *Bocage* was a general term describing the network of extremely dense hedgerows (often up to 16ft tall and far too thick for a tank to penetrate) growing out of steep banks that surrounded an irregular patchwork of small fields, cut through with winding streams, paths, causeways, and sunken roads. (Archives Normandie, 1939-1945/Wikimedia/Public Domain)

Merderet

Neuville-
au-Plain

Amfreville

Sainte-
Mère-Église

2 | II | 505 (-)

A | I | 505

La Fière

Cauquigny

La Fière
Bridge

4

II | 1057 | 3

1 | A/505

3 | A/505

3 | II | 505 (-)

1

1/100

Manoir

B/505

2 | A/505

2

Chef-du-Pont

to Saint-Sauveur-
le-Vicomte

I | 507 (-)

N

0   750yd

0   750m

Carquebut

INTO COMBAT

Lieutenant John Dolan, commanding A/505th, remembered:

> We hit our drop zone right on the nose, because within 20 minutes to half an
> hour, I knew our exact location ... We had the usual problems of reorganization
> in the dark; however, about an hour before dawn, Company A moved out from
> the drop zone with about 90 percent of the men accounted for. (This was not
> due to luck alone, but to the cooperation of my officers and non-coms [non-
> commissioned officers] and, last but not least, training. Men who have to fight in
> the night should be trained in night-time fighting, not just taken on a night march
> and digging fox holes.) (Dolan 1959)

For 91. Luftlande-Division the first hours of the invasion brought nothing
but confusion. The division's commander, Generalleutnant Wilhelm Falley,
was attending a map exercise in Rennes and thus away from his post. The
German response was also slowed by the aggressive action of small bands of
paratroopers making a nuisance of themselves, setting upon any vulnerable
enemies they found and cutting every wire they came across, hindering the flow
of information and exacerbating the impact of those reports that did manage
to filter through. One such group was led by Lieutenant Malcolm Brannen,
commander of the 508th Parachute Infantry Regiment's HQ Company, who
was trying to find out where he was from a local mill-owner when a German
staff car came barreling along the road. Its passengers were Falley and his
aide Major Joachim Bartuzat, rushing back to the 91. Luftlande-Division
command post. Brannen and his small group riddled the car with gunfire,
killing both officers. When Brannen made it to divisional headquarters and
informed Ridgway "with great glee" about his kill, the general replied: "Well,
in our present situation killing division commanders does not strike me as
being particularly hilarious. But I congratulate you. I'm glad it was a German
division commander you got" (quoted in Lord 1948: 26).

Oberstleutnant Friedrich von Criegern, who thought that 91. Luftlande-
Division's headquarters at Saint-Sauveur-le-Vicomte was under attack by a
battalion-strength unit (likely little more than an ad hoc platoon or two, at
most), noted how by 0330hrs the division could no longer communicate
with troops around Sainte-Mère-Église. In Falley's then-unexplained absence
temporary command of the division fell to Oberst Bernhard Klosterkemper.

While the staff at 91. Luftlande-Division were trying to organize
themselves, Dolan's company had gathered itself up and around an hour
before dawn it was making its way south from the drop zone toward its
objective, the eastern end of the La Fière bridge. Before long the paratroopers
came across the Sainte-Mère-Église–La Fière road and followed it westward,
coming to a halt at the edge of a field several hundred yards shy of the bridge.
An initial reconnaissance resulted in several men cut down by automatic fire;
Dolan sent his 3d Platoon to maneuver south of the road and the 2d Platoon
to do the same to the north, but both were quickly pinned down for over
an hour by fire from well-sited German machine-gun nests. Major James
McGinity, executive officer of 1/505th who had been accompanying Dolan,
was killed in the initial approach.

Members of a German patrol report back to their officer during the Normandy campaign. Life could be very dangerous in paratrooper-infested areas. 91. Luftlande-Division lost its commander to a random interdiction by a group of cutthroats from the 508th Parachute Infantry Regiment, but he was not the only one to suffer such a fate. Major Bardenschlager, commander of Panzer-Ersatz- und Ausbildungs-Abteilung 100, readied his men for action by 0900hrs on the morning of the invasion and then set off for 91. Luftlande-Division's headquarters, just over a half-mile distant; he never made it. Oberleutnant Weber, in charge of the Panzer unit's 1. Kompanie, went out to conduct his morning rounds as usual, and also never came back. The next day the commanding officer of I./ GR 1058, Major Friedrich Moch, and the headquarters staff of the *Bataillon* were gathered around a radio having an intense discussion in a sunken road when they had the misfortune to attract the attention of Lieutenant Waverly "Charlie" Wray, who was conducting a reconnaissance patrol. Wray appeared over the embankment and shouted for them to surrender: one German made a move for his pistol, so Wray shot every one of them dead with his M1 Garand rifle, pausing briefly to reload before killing another two Germans who had opened fire on him from a slit trench a little over 100yd away. (LAPI/Roger Viollet/ Getty Images)

As the morning progressed, various US units and ad hoc formations turned up at La Fière, all helping to discomfit the defenders, dislodging them first from the area around the bridge, and then from the Manoir and its outbuildings that dominated the southern side of the causeway. Most of those units moved on once again, but Dolan had the comfort of knowing that he could rely on the support of a few mortars and some machine-gun sections from HQ Company, 1/505th, about half of whom had turned up. In addition, some men from C/505th were available, as were some engineers and a platoon of B/505th.

By 1430hrs the Manoir and the eastern end of the La Fière bridge were firmly in US hands. Paratroopers crossed over the bridge and advanced around 50ft along the causeway before placing mines and retreating. A broken-down German truck was also dragged onto the road to act as an obstacle to any attempted breakthrough. Private Marcus Heim was a member of one of the two bazooka teams that Dolan had detailed to protect the bridge. While Heim and Lenold Peterson were on the Manoir side and facing Cauquigny, the second team (John Bolderson and Gordon Pryne) took position on the right side of the road; a third team was set up farther to the south to try to get a better vantage point on the causeway (Murphy 2009: 143).

The positioning of the bazooka teams was part of Dolan's organization of his defense; he set his 1st Platoon (led by Lieutenant William Oakley and Sergeant William Owens) on the northern side of the road and 3d Platoon on the south, with the 2d Platoon held in reserve some 350–400yd back from the bridge. Dolan had been glad to see the arrival of a 57mm M1 antitank gun earlier in the morning, giving his position some much-needed firepower (he had no other light weapons apart from an 81mm mortar and a couple of 60mm mortars, all of them so short of ammunition that their use was restricted to emergencies). He situated the gun next to his command post, around 150yd to the east of the bridge, just at the bend of the road. The gun, as well as a .30-caliber M1919A4 machine gun that was also sited there, had a straight line of sight along the road down to the bridge and for a farther 65yd along the causeway until it curved away to the right. The commander of 1/505th, Major Kellam, together with the battalion's S3 (operations officer), Captain Dale Roysdon, had arrived during Dolan's preparations, and agreed with his dispositions.

The confusion of the early hours that had done so much to hamper the effective control of 91. Luftlande-Division had worn off by the morning, and the division's provisional commander, Oberst Bernhard Klosterkemper, had ordered Grenadier-Regiment 1058 to attack toward Sainte-Mère-Église, while a *Kampfgruppe* made up of Grenadier-Regiment 1057 with support from Panzer-Ersatz- und Ausbildungs-Abteilung 100 was to move east along the La Fière–Sainte-Mère-Église road, seizing the bridge over the Merderet. The hastily assembled *Kampfgruppe* set off from Cauquigny, advancing along the causeway at around 1600hrs. The paratroopers could hear the tanks long before they saw them come around the bend in the road and begin to roll toward the river. Heim stated that there were three tanks, accompanied by infantry; when the commander of the lead tank emerged from the turret, the Americans opened up with every weapon at their disposal, killing the tank commander and prompting the Germans to return fire (Murphy 2009: 143).

Private First Class Dave Bullington was dug in by a hedgerow on the northern side of the bridge, and noted the advancing soldiers were bunched and staying close to the tanks (Nordyke 2010b: 175). Dolan recalled:

> My two bazooka crews called for more ammunition. Major Kellam ran up toward the bridge with a bag of rockets followed by Captain Roysdon. When they were within fifteen or twenty yards of the bridge, the Germans opened up with mortar fire on the bridge. Major Kellam was killed and Captain Roysdon was rendered unconscious from the concussion. He died later that day. (Dolan 1959)

The loss of Kellam and Roysdon, coupled with the earlier death of Major McGinity, meant that all of 1/505th's senior officers were dead, leaving Dolan, as the ranking officer, to take command of the bridge's defense.

The German advance had degenerated into a gunnery duel between the bazooka teams, the 57mm antitank gun, and the German tanks (two Renault

R 35s and a Hotchkiss H 39). The German infantry were moving haphazardly in the wake of the tanks, returning some of the heavy small-arms fire they were receiving, but there did not seem to be any serious tactical relationship between the armor and the men who were fighting alongside them. The bazookas were scoring numerous hits, as was the 57mm gun which, in its turn, was hit repeatedly, the rounds from the German tanks punching several holes through its gunshield. Sergeant Elmo Bell of C/505th recalled that as the crewmen were hit, other

A Hotchkiss (Char léger modèle 1935 modifié 1939) tank armed with the updated 37mm SA38 gun and coaxial 7.5mm Reibel machine gun, pictured during the invasion of France, 1940. The Wehrmacht captured around 550 of these French tanks, pressing them into service as training tools and armor for second-line units under the designation PzKpfw 35H 734(f) or PzKpfw 38H 735(f) (the former for H 35 models, the latter for the slightly improved N 35/9 version). Together with the Renault R 35, the H 39 made up the bulk of tanks used by Panzer-Ersatz- und Ausbildungs-Abteilung 100, and they played a significant (if unsuccessful) part in the German attempts to recapture the La Fière bridge on D-Day. (Keystone / Hulton Archive via Getty Images)

paratroopers replaced them, with some seven men being killed as they sought to crew the weapon (Bell 2003: 149). Paratroopers were cross-trained on all the weapon systems that they might come across in the field, ensuring that guns such as the vital "57" did not fall silent for the lack of a specialist.

Dolan recognized the skill of his bazooka teams, engaged in their incredibly dangerous business on the bridge: "They fired and reloaded with the precision of well-oiled machinery. Watching them made it hard to believe that this was nothing but a routine drill. I don't think that either crew wasted a shot. The first tank received several direct hits. The treads were knocked off, and within a matter of minutes it was on fire" (Dolan 1959). The two teams, having to leave their foxholes in order to get a sight picture, exhibited startling bravery in engaging the enemy armor. Seeking a good shot but with their view obscured by the trees, Heim and Peterson had to exit their foxhole and hold their fire until the last possible moment. They kept shooting at the lead tank until it was knocked out, before turning their attention to the second. By the time they could concentrate on the third tank, Heim and Peterson were running low on ammunition and so Heim rushed across the road to obtain more rockets from the second team (Murphy 2009: 143). Bolderson and Pryne were gone, having left their position after their bazooka was put out of action by gunfire. Grabbing up some leftover rockets, Heim dashed back across the road and he and Peterson engaged the third tank once more, knocking it out with the help of the 57mm gun and forcing the rest of the *Kampfgruppe* to retreat back toward Cauquigny.

Having been thwarted in a direct attack, the *Kampfgruppe* switched to '88s and mortars – the latter an effective and much-feared weapon in the hands of the well-trained German crews – and began hammering A/505th's position. Dolan observed that

> The mortar fire was very effective against the two forward platoons because of tree bursts. It took very little imagination on the part of the Krauts to figure out just where we would be dug in. As I recall, there was less than a 75-yard frontage on

Contesting La Fière, June 6, 1944

US view: Having taken possession of the La Fière bridge, Lieutenant John Dolan and A/505th find themselves at the beginning of a long, arduous fight to keep the Germans from breaking through and threatening the beachheads a few miles to the east. Paratroopers are scattered to either side of the bridge, dug-in on the slopes of the causeway; two bazooka teams are positioned at the eastern edge of the bridge, one on each side, supported by a 57mm M1 antitank gun and a .30-caliber M1919A4 machine gun 150yd down the road to the east of the bridge. Three tanks are approaching (two Renault R 35s about 20yd apart, followed by a Hotchkiss H 39 50yd farther back) supported by infantry and significant machine-gun fire, when they are engaged by the bazooka teams who have to leave their foxholes (dug in below the level of the causeway) and expose themselves to enemy fire if they are to score any hits. The German infantry scatter for cover while the first two R 35s are hit one after the other by multiple bazooka rockets and 57mm HEAT rounds, knocking them both out.

German view: As the ad hoc *Kampfgruppe* tasked with driving the Americans from the bridge comes into view, heavy US machine-gun fire forces most of the German infantry to take cover. The small unit of German tanks forges ahead, two Renault R 35s in the vanguard with a Hotchkiss H 39 coming along behind them. As the tanks close with the bridge the first vehicle is hit multiple times and, choking in smoke and flame, veers off to the left trying to escape the causeway. Supporting fire from German machine guns and infantry sprays the bridge and its environs, but to no apparent effect. A small group of German riflemen and a light-machine-gun team are being led forward by a determined NCO using the advance of the second R 35 as cover, but the incoming fire is too treacherous for them to risk getting too close to the tank. Even as they try to advance, the second tank is in a fierce engagement with the bazooka teams and the 57mm M1 antitank gun, but it has taken numerous hits and now it too is starting to burn.

either side of the bridge from where we could effectively defend, so they could throw their mortar fire in our general direction with good results. (Dolan 1959)

Eventually the firing died down as night approached, with no more tanks or infantry making an appearance on the causeway.

The relative calm gifted by the night did not last long into the following day, soon giving way to increasing shellfire that was the herald of another attack. The bombardment heralded another attack by a large number of German infantry supported by a pair of tanks in the vanguard and another pair bringing up the rear. Dolan checked on his 57mm gun and found it abandoned with its firing mechanism missing. Fortunately the gunners, under their own initiative, returned in the nick of time and started sending HEAT rounds at the lead tanks, knocking out both of them. With no way along the causeway due to the pile-up of vehicles to their front, the two remaining tanks at the rear of the German column withdrew, but the infantry flooded forward, using the piles of wrecked armor that littered the causeway as cover. They were beaten back by small-arms fire, but their place was quickly taken by another pounding from the German artillery, 12cm mortars, and '88s. Severely wounded in the back, Lieutenant Oakley managed to get himself to cover, but soon died of his wounds. Fearing another attack, Owens began crawling from position to position, gathering up all the spare ammunition and grenades that he could find from the dead and wounded.

82d Airborne Division paratroopers relaxing after liberating the village of Sainte-Mère-Église in Normandy, June 8, 1944. A/505th had started D-Day with 137 men. By D+2 the company was down to 66, including 20 walking wounded. The 57mm gun, with its battered gunshield, had been put out of action by shellfire sometime during the afternoon's fighting. A/505th had blocked every attempt by the enemy to take the bridge, no German having crossed it since the morning of D-Day. With the rest of 1/505th, the company was withdrawn the following day; the job of taking the western side and the causeway beyond it would fall to elements of the 507th Parachute Infantry Regiment together with the glider infantry of the 2/325th and 3/325th. (FPG/Getty Images)

The German renewed their fire on the position; the relentless shelling was accompanied by another infantry attack, pushing closer and closer. The 1st Platoon, linchpin to A/504th's defensive line, was taking a hammering, with only 15 men left. Ammunition was running low, and weapons were malfunctioning. Owens' machine gun overheated, and so he took over first Private McClatchy's BAR and then a second machine gun, this time with no tripod; he recalled that the enemy came within 25yd of overrunning his position (Gavin 1978: 114).

Owens had thought the situation untenable, detailing Murphy to find Dolan and ask permission to withdraw, but Dolan refused. Owens barely had time to digest the order to remain at his post when the firing died down and a Red Cross flag was seen waving above the German position on the causeway; they wanted a half-hour ceasefire in which to gather their wounded. Owens, who had worked his way forward to get a better vantage point on the causeway, noted that it took roughly two hours for the Germans to retrieve their wounded, after which the shelling resumed; the enemy did not attempt another infantry attack (Nordyke 2010b: 180).

91. Luftlande-Division's casualties fighting on the Cotentin peninsula were significant, the unit losing 2,212 men to all causes in the first six days of the invasion, and by the end of the month it was reduced to four battered *Kampfgruppen* of variable strength (Zetterling 2000: 240). The crippling losses could not be made good, and the division ceased to exist on August 10.

Nijmegen

September 19–20, 1944

BACKGROUND TO BATTLE

The 82d Airborne Division under Brigadier General James Gavin had made an excellent landing, dropping in daylight in locations around Grave–Nijmegen. The division's three parachute infantry regiments immediately set about their business. The 504th Parachute Infantry Regiment (Colonel Reuben Tucker) seized all but one of its objectives – bridges across the Maas–Waal Canal as well as a major prize in the shape of the Grave bridge, stormed from both ends and secured with surprising ease. The 505th Parachute Infantry Regiment (Colonel William Ekman) dropped south of Groesbeek, taking the nearby heights and setting up defenses against any incursion from the Reichswald Forest. The 508th Parachute Infantry Regiment (Colonel Roy Lindquist) dropped to the southeast of Nijmegen, securing the nearby high ground and setting up a defensive perimeter, but it failed in its third task – to move along the riverbank into Nijmegen and seize the road and railroad bridges. The attack on the Waalbrug road bridge and Spoorbrug railroad bridge had not been given the highest priority, so the chance to seize them before the Germans knew what was happening slipped away.

Many of the Wehrmacht forces facing the Allies in Operation *Market Garden* were a confusing mixture of some front-line formations and a panoply of rear-echelon units (including military-police detachments, occupation forces, training and replacement units, and the like). The plethora of ad hoc and replacement units in the area is amply demonstrated by the fact that on

An aerial view of the 655yd-long Waalbrug road bridge across the Waal River taken in 1944 (a reconnaissance photo judging by the lack of damage evident to the bridge and its surrounding areas). The Dutch underground offered crucial intelligence, informing the Allied planners that they would not face German opposition until within a few hundred yards of the Waalbrug; the strong defenses around the bridge itself included antitank guns (Jacobus 1992: 349). The capture of the Waalbrug was essential for the success of Operation *Market Garden* as it connected the southern and northern parts of the city of Nijmegen across the Waal – a distributary channel of the Rhine and the main waterway between Rotterdam and Germany. In addition, the Spoorbrug railroad bridge 1,100yd to the west of the Waalbrug was also an important tactical objective. The 82d Airborne Division had a daunting task: to land in and hold a 25-mile perimeter as well as take nine bridges, five over canals and four over rivers. In addition to defending its landing zones around Nijmegen, the division had to secure the Groesbeek Heights, an area of ground located to the southeast of Nijmegen whose wooded slopes rose up just over 300ft, forming a broad plateau, and which would provide a strong defensive position against any German attacks that were expected to develop from the Reichswald Forest to the east. (HMSO/Wikimedia/Public Domain)

the first day of the landings the 82d Airborne Division captured 156 German troops from a total of 28 different units, hardly any of which were standard front-line combat formations (Zaloga 2014: 17). Unfortunately for the Allies there were also better-trained, battle-hardened units within striking distance, including the much-reduced Panzer divisions of SS-Obergruppenführer Wilhelm Bittrich's II. SS-Panzerkorps.

The German forces in Nijmegen were negligible, and were quickly reinforced with Kampfgruppe *Henke*, led by Oberst Fritz Henke, commander of Fallschirmjäger-Lehr-Regiment 1. His force was based around the headquarters company of Fallschirm-Panzer-Ersatz- und Ausbildungs-Regiment *Hermann Göring* including its Unteroffiziers-Lehr-Kompanie 29, along with three companies from Ersatz-Bataillon 6 from Wehrkreis VI (Zaloga 2014: 48). Henke's command moved into Nijmegen on September 17, augmenting the city's existing forces (Hermann Göring Kompanie *Runge*, an NCO school company, two companies of railroad guards/police reservists, and an antiaircraft battery of mixed 2cm and 8.8cm guns). The total strength of his newly combined forces ran to around 750 men, nowhere near enough to fend off the encroaching battalions of the 82d Airborne Division.

Realizing how crucial it was to stop any Allied relief force breaking through at Nijmegen, orders from II. SS-Panzerkorps were issued at 1730hrs on September 17 to 10. SS-Panzer-Division *Frundsberg* stationed near Arnhem. The division was to move against the forces landed at Nijmegen, seizing and holding the bridges and preventing a link-up between the Allies' airborne and ground forces. At midnight on September 17/18, several strong elements from the much-depleted 10. SS-Panzer-Division were diverted from Arnhem, led by Kampfgruppe *Reinhold*, commanded by SS-Sturmbannführer Leo Reinhold, who set up his command on the northern bank of the Waal. The main unit sent into Nijmegen was a *Kampfgruppe* built around I./SS-PzGrenRgt 22 under the command of

A close-up view of the 2cm Flakvierling 38. Autocannon such as this and the 2cm FlaK 30/38 (the single-barreled version) were used in the defense of the bridges at Nijmegen, including sites on the railroad bridge and the Hof van Holland fort. Though theoretically an antiaircraft weapon, it was often mounted on halftracks and pressed into use against ground targets to provide immediate support for infantry attacks, as it was against 3/504th during that unit's treacherous Waal crossing. Being under such fire while exposed in canvas boats was bracing, to say the least. Fire came from gun positions on the railroad bridge around 1,100yd to the east, as well as from the parapets of the Hof van Holland on the northern shore. (Nik Cornish at www.stavka.org.uk)

SS-Hauptsturmführer Karl-Heinz Euling. Euling's force started arriving in Nijmegen from midday on September 18, establishing a command post near the Valkhof citadel between the two bridges and with its attention centered on the Hunnerpark and the southern entrance to the Waalbrug. The defense of the Spoorbrug to the west would mainly fall to Kampfgruppe *Henke*. In addition, Kampfgruppe *Baumgärtel* (made up of engineers from SS-Pionier-Bataillon 10, reinforced with part of an *SS-Ersatz-Abteilung*) took up position in and around the Valkhof. These groups were augmented by a variety of antiaircraft (2cm, 3.7cm, and 8.8cm) and antitank guns, the latter including four 5cm PaK 38 pieces in the Hunnerpark. The divisional artillery was positioned on the north side of the Waal, including SS-Panzer-Artillerie Regiment 10, all the available infantry guns, as well as SS-Hauptsturmführer Oskar Schwappacher's V. Abteilung/SS-Artillerie-Ausbildung- und Ersatz-Regiment (forward observers from Schwappacher's 21. Batterie were ensconced in Nijmegen to ensure that they were able to direct the fire of the regiment's guns with the utmost speed and precision). By September 19, when the Americans decided to mount an attack on the bridges through the town, there were over 3,000 German troops holding Nijmegen, its bridges, and the northern bank of the Waal, most of them battle-hardened Waffen-SS personnel.

By September 19 it was clear that a concerted attack would be needed to break through to the bridges. Gavin, in concert with Lieutenant-General Sir Brian Horrocks, freshly arrived with his British XXX Corps, decided on an assault through the city that would be conducted by Lieutenant Colonel Ben Vandervoort's 2/505th in concert with No. 3 Squadron, 2nd Grenadier Guards

A company of Waffen-SS troops mustering, Fall 1944. The SS men encountered by 2/504th in Nijmegen and 3/504th on the northern bank of the Waal would fight hard, giving little quarter. (ullstein bild/ullstein bild via Getty Images)

and No. 2 Company, 1st Grenadier Guards; the advance was to develop along two lines, the left aimed at the Spoorbrug and the right at the Waalbrug. The Spoorbrug attack was to be carried out by D/505th, supported by a troop of tanks from No. 3 Squadron, 2nd Grenadier Guards and one platoon of infantry from No. 2 Company, 1st Grenadier Guards. The Waalbrug attack was to be conducted by E/505th and F/505th as well as 2/505th's HQ Company, supported by three troops of tanks of No. 3 Squadron, 2nd Grenadier Guards, and three platoons of No. 2 Company, 1st Grenadier Guards.

Armored elements of the 2nd Grenadier Guards together with paratroopers from Lieutenant Colonel Ben Vandervoort's 2/505th prepare to move off into Nijmegen, September 19, 1944. (Keystone/Getty Images)

MAP KEY

1 1345hrs, September 19: 2/505th, No. 3 Squadron, 2nd Grenadier Guards, and No. 2 Company, 1st Grenadier Guards launch a two-pronged attack through Nijmegen, aimed at capturing the southern ends of the Spoorbrug railroad bridge and Waalbrug road bridge. Both British columns run into fierce resistance that blunts their progress.

2 1500hrs, September 20: The first wave of 3/504th (H/504th, I/504th, and some headquarters elements) under the command of Major Julian Cook sets off from the shore near the Gelderland power plant and begins crossing the Waal under intense German machine-gun, 2cm, mortar, and artillery fire.

3 1530hrs, September 20: The survivors of the Waal crossing charge the dike embankment in scattered groups, killing or routing all its defenders. Defensive positions are set up to the west and north, while individual American groups move onward to the bridges.

4 c.1600hrs, September 20: 1st Lieutenant James Megellas with a handful of men attacks the Hof van Holland, forcing its defenders to retreat inside, thus enabling his men to destroy the 2cm gun emplacements along the fort's parapet.

5 1700hrs, September 20: The northern end of the Spoorbrug is overrun by elements of H/504th and I/504th, cutting off an avenue of retreat for German troops fleeing Nijmegen.

6 1915hrs, September 20: After overwhelming the defenders at the northern end of the Waalbrug, US paratroopers subdue all remaining German troops positioned in the bridge's superstructure, opening the way for an armored advance by the Grenadier Guards.

7 2230hrs, September 20: SS-Hauptsturmführer Karl-Heinz Euling abandons his defensive position at the Valkhof citadel, leading a surreptitious breakout of his *Kampfgruppe*, which manages to make it across the river and back to German lines.

Battlefield environment

Martha Gellhorn, who was with the 82d Airborne Division in the Netherlands, noted that the exposed roads offered no cover, with the Hof van Holland dominating the approaches to both of the bridges (Gellhorn 1944: 12). The task of crossing the Waal would prove to be the most formidable undertaking of the battle. Recalling the view from the Gelderland power plant on the southern shore, Captain T. Moffatt Burriss of I/504th stated that across the swiftly flowing river, 300yd across, he could see level ground that stretched for about 900yd before meeting a 15ft-tall dike with a road running along it. Burriss and his comrades could make out German machine guns along the roadway and mortar and artillery positions beyond it (Burriss 2000: 109–10).

A view of Nijmegen and the Waalbrug road bridge after the fighting, taken on September 28, 1944, showing the extent of the destruction caused by artillery fire. The trees visible by the southern end of the Waalbrug (at the far right of the picture) are part of the Hunnerpark, which marked the farthest advance of the initial US patrols on September 18. The old tower located in the Hunnerpark – the Belvedere – was used as an observation post by Kampfgruppe *Euling* in the battle. (US Archiv ARCWEB/ Wikimedia/Public Domain)

to Arnhem

KG
Reinhold

3

Hof van
Holland

4

Gelderland
Power Station

Waal

2

504

H   504

HQ   3/504

5

6

7

Spoorbrug

Waalbrug

Hunnerpark

KG
Henke

Valkhof

KG
Euling

Belvedere
Tower

KG
Baumgärtel

3/2 GG

D   505

F   505

E   505

2   1 GG (-)

3   2 GG (-)

1

2/1 GG

HQ   2/505

1

N

0   500yd

0   500m

INTO COMBAT

Setting off at 1345hrs, the two Allied combined-arms columns encountered extremely fierce resistance, slowing their advance to a crawl. Fighting devolved into close-quarter actions, with the paratroopers, British tanks, and infantry having to work hard to support each other in the face of highly accurate fire from '88s and PaK guns, supported by intense artillery barrages. Vandervoort's paratroopers were fighting from house to house, often having to dig through common walls to avoid the danger of moving from door to door. It was clear that the intense fight being put up by the various *Kampfgruppen* in the city meant that reaching the bridges would not be a quick affair. By that evening Gavin had decided that the best way to wrongfoot the defenders would be to send a force across the Waal, enveloping the northern bridgeheads while the southern bridgeheads were still being hammered by the Grenadier Guards and Vandervoort's 2/505th.

Gavin had ideally wanted to cross the river at night, but time and logistics were against him. The crossing, to be carried out by Major Julian Cook's 3/504th now that it had been freed up from defensive duties on the Grave by XXX Corps, would have to be conducted in daylight, ideally at dawn on September 20. The 82d Airborne Division's engineers had no boats with them, but Horrocks told Gavin that XXX Corps did, though they were some way behind the corps' lead elements. They were originally scheduled to arrive at 0800hrs, but difficulties in transporting the boats along a route jammed with XXX Corps vehicles meant that it was 1400hrs before they actually arrived. The "Goatley" boats were not particularly inspiring collapsible canvas-walled affairs, but there was nothing better available (the civilian boats having been cleared from the riverbanks by the Germans), and they worked; each boat was to be crewed by three engineers (drawn from C/307th AEB) and could accommodate 11 passengers (though some managed more).

A .30-caliber M1A1 carbine with folding stock and a 15-round magazine; the example shown here is one of the early production models, identifiable by its "L"-shaped rear flip sight and the lack of a bayonet lug. The M1A1 was the only individual weapon specifically designed for paratroopers, and was issued from late 1942, initially to engineers, though later to other specialists and officers. The M1 carbine (and its folding-stock variant) was designed to fill the need for a personal defense weapon for troops who were not front-line infantrymen (such as truck drivers, messengers, and artillerymen) and who therefore did not need the encumbrance of a full-length battle rifle, but who still required more than the short-range capabilities of a .45-caliber M1911A1 pistol or Thompson SMG. The M1A1 was chambered for a lighter cartridge (.30 Carbine as opposed to the M1 Garand rifle's more substantial .30-06), and would prove to be a versatile, if not universally popular weapon. (NRA Museums, NRAmuseums.com)

The plan for 3/504th was relatively straightforward in design, at least. The assault over the river by 3/504th would be launched around 2,200yd to the west of the Waalbrug, setting off from the banks next to the site of the old Gelderland power plant. The 26 boats would ferry two rifle companies and the battalion HQ company to the far bank of the river 2 miles to the west of the Waalbrug in two waves. The first wave would comprise H/504th (Captain Carl Kappel), I/504th (Captain T. Moffatt Burriss), and elements of 3/504th's HQ Company (Major Julian Cook); the second wave would comprise G/504th (Captain Fred Thomas) and the remainder of 3/504th's HQ Company. Such a perilous undertaking would need all the help it could get, Captain Kappel recalling:

> Tanks of the 2nd Irish Guards would support the crossings by fire from positions on the dike. The 2nd Battalion, 504 Parachute Infantry, would support the crossings by fire from positions along the dike. The 376 Parachute Field Artillery was in direct support, to be supplemented with all available British artillery [which was] arriving constantly. All artillery was to fire a ten-minute concentration on the target area. Dive bombers and rocket-firing Typhoons were to bomb and strafe from 1445 to 1455. The area [was] to be smoked at 1455 by artillery and mortars. (75mm howitzer and 81mm mortar [fire was] not as satisfactory as desired.) Tanks were to fill in blanks of the smoke to the limit of their capacity. H-Hour was set at 1500 hours. (Kappel 1947: 26)

Once across the river the US rifle companies would need to fight their way across an expanse of fields toward the embankment of the dike road, where they would regroup and deploy defensive blocking patrols to the west and north to interdict any possible counterattacks. Captain Henry Keep of I/504th wrote how the rest of the force was to pivot east and advance parallel to the

German soldiers from the *Großdeutschland* Division load their 8.8cm Raketenpanzerbüchse 54, known as the *Ofenrohr* ("stovepipe") or *Panzerschreck* ("tank terror"). Developed from captured examples of the US M1 bazooka rocket launcher, the *Panzerschreck* was a potent antitank weapon; by 1944 each rifle company ideally would field two sections, each with six men and three *Panzerschreck* launchers. Its effective range was 165yd, with teams advised to engage their targets at a minimum of 30–35yd. Antitank companies that were newly raised or which had lost their guns would often find themselves allocated recoilless rocket weapons instead, with around 9–12 *Panzerschreck* or *Panzerfaust* ("tank fist") weapons replacing each gun. (ullstein bild/ullstein bild via Getty Images)

river towards the Spoorbrug, subduing enemy resistance along the way before storming the bridge; once the Spoorbrug was in hand they were to move on and do the same with the Waalbrug – a formidable task (Nordyke 2008: 225).

Major Cook, who had decided to cross with the first wave, tried to keep up the spirits of his men (and himself), giving words of encouragement to them as they filed through the staging areas. Despite the smokescreen and supporting artillery barrage, the Germans began firing on them as soon as they broke cover and manhandled their awkward burdens toward the water's edge. One by one the boats made it to the river where the desperate struggle to row them across as fast as possible began. Many paratroopers aided the engineer crews in the work of rowing, Sergeant Jimmy Shields of H/504th remembering how he used the butt of his BAR to paddle (Megellas 2003: 143).

The effects of German fire on men in such an exposed situation was terrible, especially the horrendous wounds caused by the direct fire of 2cm antiaircraft guns that literally blew men to pieces. Incessant machine-gun fire raked the river, complemented by mortars once the boats were about halfway across. When a mortar achieved a direct hit on one boat, the explosion destroyed the vessel and left half of 1st Lieutenant James Megellas' platoon and their engineer crewmen floundering in the water, weighed down with weapons and ammunition, without life vests, and nobody able to come to their rescue.

Of the 26 boats that attempted the first crossing, 13 made the far bank, of which 11 returned to pick up G/504th and the remainder of the HQ Company. Continuing attrition meant that it took five crossings to

shuttle the second wave across the river, after which only five boats were left. The first wave had been severely hit, with only around 125 men making it to shore in any fit state to fight. The riverbank offered little respite to those fortunate few who had survived the crossing, and as soon as they could small groups of paratroopers moved inland. The dike road was stormed by disparate groups of paratroopers, furious for vengeance and in no mood to put up with any resistance. Upon the orders of Captain Burriss the men showered the reverse side of the dike with grenades that broke the German resistance. When the Germans tried to surrender they were offered no quarter by the enraged paratroopers (Burriss 2000: 115). Some troopers took up defensive positions to the north and west, while the rest of H/504th and I/504th moved off in small groups toward the Spoorbrug. One such group of around 30 men included Major Cook and Captain Keep, who recalled how constant pressure and aggressive action kept the defenders off-balance, rolling them back wherever they were met (Nordyke 2008: 247).

At the same time, Megellas and a small band of troopers had worked their way along the northern bank of the Waal until they were within striking distance of the Hof van Holland, an old fort turned into a defensive emplacement that had contributed to the punishment his company endured as it crossed the Waal. Megellas directed his men to concentrate their fire upon the 2cm antiaircraft guns and machine guns until the German gunners were suppressed, at which point the Americans surged forward toward the moat, hurling grenades into the fort (Megellas 2003: 152–53). The attack

Dutch civilians welcoming some US paratroopers in the countryside around Arnhem. This paratrooper is likely from the 82d Airborne Division and appears to be a grenadier (there would usually be two men per rifle squad designated as such), judging by the fact that he seems to be armed with a Springfield M1903 rifle fitted with a barrel spigot to accept a 22mm rifle grenade. Although a rifle-grenade mount had been developed for the M1 Garand by 1943 (the rifle grenade launcher, M7), Springfields continued to be used by many grenadiers until the end of the war, as well as for sniping (the M1903A4 variant – the M1 Garand's action made mounting a telescopic sight impractical, so the bolt-action Springfield was retained in that role). (Mondadori Portfolio via Getty Images)

Storming the Hof van Holland

In order to seize the strategically vital bridges over the Waal, two companies of 3/504th have crossed the river in broad daylight, losing half their number in the teeth of ferocious enemy resistance. Scattered bands of men have scrambled ashore, joined up with one another, and proceeded to drive through the German defenses on the northern bank of the river. One such group, not much more than an ad hoc squad, was commanded by 1st Lieutenant James Megellas; striking east toward the Waal bridgeheads, Megellas came up against one of his battalion's key objectives, the Hof van Holland (also called Fort Lent), a fortified position that has been pouring 2cm gun and machine-gun fire into the paratroopers still crossing the river and whose location meant that it could enfilade any attack on the northern approaches to the railroad and river

bridges. The fort was a circular earthwork of hard-packed dirt surrounded by a moat, capped with numerous emplacements for antiaircraft guns. Suppressing the fire from the crest of the fort, Megellas together with 11 of his men worked their way around to the fort's southern flank where a causeway led into the heart of the position. He sent two men across the causeway to the fort's entrance where a firefight and an exchange of stick grenades and No. 82 "Gammon" bombs (a type of grenade made from an explosive-filled stockinette bag that detonated on sharp contact) broke out with the defenders in the inner courtyard, prompting Megellas and his remaining men to charge across the causeway and scale the Hof van Holland's walls in an attempt to gain the parapet and destroy the gun emplacements for good.

disabled the antiaircraft guns and forced the defenders to take shelter, though it took some time to pacify fully. Captain Carl Kappel of H/504th noted that "the fort remained a definite problem all afternoon, as it consisted of many layers, until it was completely cleared by the 1st Battalion later in the day and occupied as the regimental CP. The 1st Battalion took some 30 prisoners, plus inflicting numerous casualties before the fort was [written off as] captured" (Kappel 1947: 31).

By 1700hrs groups of paratroopers (including one led by Captain Kappel) were reaching the Spoorbrug, where hard fighting by the defenders made the going difficult, but one strongpoint after another was overrun or neutralized. A small force of 19 paratroopers led by Lieutenant Edward Sims (executive officer, H/504th) and Lieutenant Richard LaRiviere (2d Platoon, H/504th) overwhelmed disparate groups of defenders to take up position at the northern end of the Spoorbrug, where they arrived just in time to see a force of up to 500 German troops – knowing they were about to be cut off and hard-pressed by the armor of the Grenadier Guards and men of D/504th – trying to escape across the railroad bridge from the ruins of Nijmegen to the south. Kappel watched as

These units made several counterattacks across the bridge, which were easily dealt with … Many Germans, now hopelessly cut off, attempted to escape by jumping from the bridge. The men were shooting them in the air until stopped by me, due to the shortage of ammunition. Two [captured] German machine guns were mounted to sweep the long axis of the bridge, and the German situation was now hopeless. One of the German prisoners who could understand English, was ordered out on the bridge to tell the Germans to cross to the south side and surrender. He was shot by the Germans pinned on the bridge. They were again swept by machine gun fire, and many leaped from the bridge, even though they were not over the river. None surrendered at this time. (Kappel 1947: 34)

Some 267 bodies were recovered from the Spoorbrug, with many more lost in the waters below. Sims' platoon sergeant, Staff Sergeant David Rosencrantz, said that such an action "was typical of what went on during the battle of

Nijmegen bridge ... [it] did not last as long as Sicily, Salerno and Anzio, but it was tougher and bloodier while it lasted" (quoted in McQuaid 1944).

With the Spoorbrug firmly in hand, LaRiviere ordered Sims to hold the position while he joined up with Burriss and struck out eastward along the dike toward the Waalbrug, clearing houses as they went. Breaking into two groups, Burriss' force occupied the northern end of the Waalbrug with little initial effort, though his men were soon coming under fire from troops positioned on the bridge itself. Other units started arriving to add their support, including Megellas and his handful of men who had fought their way through more tough resistance after their suppression of the Hof van Holland.

On the south of the river the constant attrition meted out by Vandervoort's 2/505th and the Grenadier Guards had ground Kampfgruppe *Euling* backward, house by house, block by block, and by 1620hrs a concerted Allied attack was launched to try to drive through to the Waalbrug. Though still intensely dangerous, the worst of the German resistance at the southern bridgehead was shattered, allowing paratroopers and tanks to begin mopping up.

By 1915hrs the northern end of the Waalbrug was somewhat precariously held by handfuls of exhausted paratroopers who were almost out of ammunition, but fortunately the enemy had neither the organization nor the will to launch a counterattack. Once the Shermans of the Grenadier Guards began rolling across the smoke-wreathed bridge around 1940hrs, knocking out a sole defending 8.8cm gun, it was effectively over. By 2230hrs that evening it was clear to Euling that with the northern bridgeheads gone there was nothing more that could be done, except to save the 60-odd *Panzergrenadiere* who were all that was left of his command.

Sherman tanks crossing the newly captured Waalbrug at Nijmegen in the Netherlands. The bridges fell on September 20, but progress to Arnhem, just over 9 miles away by road, was not quick, much to the disgust of several of the officers of 3/504th, who thought the sacrifices just endured by their battalion were being wasted due to the timorousness of their British allies. There were still strong German forces in the area, including Kampfgruppe *Reinhold* at the village of Lent 1.5 miles north of Nijmegen, augmented by troops coming from Arnhem freed up by the collapse of Lieutenant-Colonel John Frost's 2nd Battalion, The Parachute Regiment. In addition, the fastest route along the main road was also by far the most dangerous: it was laid on an elevated embankment, with tank-bogging fields of polder on either side, funneling any armored column into a "suicide skyline" (Zaloga 2014: 72) that would offer a feast for German antitank guns. (Keystone/Getty Images)

Analysis

SICILY

The scattering of the 505th Parachute Regimental Combat Team across such a large area obviously blunted much of the unit's combat effectiveness, but it had the benefit of panicking the island's defenders who were overwhelmed with reports of paratroopers dropping over hundreds of square miles, as well as throwing some of those paratroopers into the path of Panzer-Division *Hermann Göring*'s two-pronged advance on the US beachheads. Without doubt the paratroopers' high level of training combined with aggression and a willingness to seize the initiative in the face of uncertain odds made a material difference to the chances of German success. General der Fallschirmtruppe Kurt Student, commander of Germany's *Fallschirmjäger*, believed that the Allies owed their victory in the Sicily operation to the paratroopers' efforts to prevent Panzer-Division *Hermann Göring* from reaching the beachhead, thereby allowing the build-up of those Allied forces landed by sea to the point where they could resist a German counterattack (Gavin 1980: 16).

For Panzer-Division *Hermann Göring*, freshly reconstituted after its disastrous losses in North Africa, the Sicilian campaign was something of a misfire. The division's notional elite status resided in its name and cuff-title alone, most of its men and officers being poorly trained in the complexities of armored warfare, with particular shortcomings among more senior officers who repeatedly failed to take the initiative, press home attacks with enough aggression, or see clearly what needed to be done to forestall the Allies from establishing their beachheads. The Tiger company (never really a good fit in the rough hills and narrow village streets of Sicily) was symptomatic: it was misused tactically, the troops of Panzergrenadier-Regiment *Hermann Göring* did not know how to work with the Panzers effectively (or how to protect them), and most of the losses were avoidable (the result of logistical blunders about which the division had been specifically forewarned). Major Gierga, commander of Panzer-Abteilung 215, attributed the failings to a mixture of arrogance and incompetence (Jentz 1996: 107).

Operation *Husky* provided the airborne forces with many lessons to learn, not the least of which was that drastic improvements were needed in the techniques and practice of delivering the men to their drop zones. Despite the paratroopers' effectiveness in resisting the German advance, it became clear that quick assembly and organization was crucial if paratroop units were to have a reasonable chance of success in achieving their objectives. In future they would also ideally be used as a strategic asset, and in much greater numbers, to ensure the maximum possible impact upon the enemy.

NORMANDY

The failure of the German defenses in Normandy was a mixture of the strategic and the logistical. They had thought to develop an "ocean front" (the defense of the beaches) and a "land front" (the defense of inland areas from airborne attack), the strategy being to stop the two anticipated wings of an Allied invasion joining up. In a postwar debriefing some of the German officers involved noted the limitations of such a strategy:

> During the invasion, however, the Allies did not oblige by landing their troops inland beyond the land front, but landed them either into it or between the two fronts. Furthermore, since the German land front was occupied by insufficient forces because of a shortage of personnel and since it had not been adequately developed, its value was illusory. As a matter of fact, the obstacles, such as the flooding, at some points even protected Allied airborne troops against attacks by German reserves. (PAM 20-232 1951: 27)

Paratroopers advance cautiously through a French cemetery at Saint-Marcouf, June 6, 1944. Postwar analysis by German officers of how to defend against airborne attacks identified several key areas, one of which was a rapid response even though (due to the scarcity of good or timely information) one could not be sure if it was the right response aimed at the right target. "It is a unique characteristic of airborne operations that the moments of greatest weakness of the attacker and of the defender occur simultaneously. The issue is therefore decided by three factors: who has the better nerves; who takes the initiative first; and who acts with greater determination. In this connection, the attacker always has the advantage of being free to choose the time and place of attack, and he therefore knows in advance when the moment of weakness will occur, whereas the defender must wait to find out where and when the attack will take place" (PAM 20-232 1951: 28). (MPI/ Getty Images)

The bodies of dead German soldiers near Saint-Fromond, a few miles to the southeast of Carentan. Initiative and aggression would prove to be the key to many of the paratroopers' successes. James Gavin observed that the violent shock with which most firefights began often left its participants numbed, allowing those who retained their wits and initiative to attack aggressively, forcing the issue in their favor. (Archives Normandie, 1939-1945/Wikimedia/Public Domain)

The attack on its command post (probably carried out by a few platoons rather than the battalion the Germans assumed) as well as Generalleutnant Wilhelm Falley's death certainly damaged the ability of 91. Luftlande-Division to respond to the invasion. Added to this were its shortages of equipment (including anything resembling modern armor) and its general inexperience in conducting complex combat operations (combating a divisional-strength airborne incursion across dozens of square miles of rough country in the middle of the night is certainly complex), both of which were grave disadvantages. As for support, those German units not in the immediate vicinity of the landings found it difficult to react quickly due to inexperience and a lack of mobility that was caused by a lack of vehicles of every type, as well as a shortage of spare parts and fuel. In such circumstances the strength and aggression of the German response was impressive, but its corollary came in the high number of casualties suffered and the virtual annihilation of 91. Luftlande-Division as a fighting force. Ultimately the conclusion of senior German officers involved in the campaign was that

> The German reserves were almost completely tied down by the airlandings, making it impossible to launch effective counterattacks against the amphibious assault. Consequently, the attackers were able to gain a foothold on the coast and, within a short time, to establish contact with the airborne elements. The tactical objective of establishing a bridgehead was thus accomplished despite German countermeasures. (PAM 20-232 1951: 34)

The men of the 82d Airborne Division, extremely well trained and including many combat veterans of the Sicilian campaign, exhibited initiative, independent thinking, and a high level of aggression, all of which proved to be vitally important in the first few confusing hours on the ground. Generalleutnant Karl Wilhelm von Schlieben of 709. Infanterie-Division observed that "Even when taking into account the strong superiority in materiel and personnel, and preparations lasting several years without interference, together with the absence of the German Luftwaffe, one must admit that it was an immensely efficient Allied organization which brought about these results within a short space of time and during the short nights of the month of June" (Schlieben 1954: 29).

NIJMEGEN

In Operation *Market Garden* ambition outstripped reality, but not by much, with luck, or the lack of it, playing its part. The German analysis of their victories in the Netherlands, given by General der Flakartillerie August Schmidt, is succinct and accurate: "the Germans repeatedly succeeded in causing critical situations which delayed the advance of the Allied ground forces. Specifically, they managed to hold the bridge at Nijmegen for another four days, thus preventing the enemy from establishing contact with the northernmost airheads at Arnhem" (PAM 20-232 1951: 35). XXX Corps' armored thrust progressed on a narrow front, allowing German forces to concentrate their counterattacking efforts along its flanks and thereby slowing overall progress, which was compounded by the inability of the 82d Airborne Division to secure the Nijmegen bridges quickly, creating a disastrous bottleneck.

The failure to take the Waalbrug on the first day was a critical mistake. There was a strong sense among the British planners (adopted by Gavin) that the Reichswald Forest was a nest of German armor that could prove fatal to any attempt to hold Nijmegen, and though there was a real threat from that quarter it was not the key objective – the bridges over the Grave, the Maas–Waal Canal, and the Waal were. Time and again surprise, speed, and aggression are cited as key elements of any successful airborne operation, and there is little doubt that greater boldness would have secured the Waalbrug in the first hours of the landing, much as the bridge at Grave had been.

That being said, such a seizure would have been the result of a gamble taken by elite troops, not one borne out by deliberate planning. Gavin was well aware that the best way to take a bridge was to grab both ends at once, but it seems probable that with his division tasked to defend a frontage that was already much larger than it could comfortably handle, to project the initial drop over the river would be an invitation to disaster. Gavin decided that once safely on the ground and aware of the dispositions of the enemy, if a battalion could be spared, it had to be committed to the bridge as quickly as possible (Gavin 1978: 150). This rather diffident decision, compounded by the confused and ineffective attempts of 1/508th to assault the southern end of the Waalbrug, gave the defenders the breathing space they so desperately needed to organize and reinforce their scanty defenses; surprise, speed, and aggression were qualities the men of 9. SS-Panzer Division *Hohenstaufen* and 10. SS-Panzer-Division *Frundsberg* could also display when called upon to do so. The tenacious heroism displayed by the 82d Airborne Division in the assault on the city, and particularly in the river crossing and subsequent capture of the Waalbrug, was beyond doubt, but it was not enough to save the British, little more than 9 miles away at Arnhem.

Aftermath

Airborne warfare required significant investments in manpower, training, equipment, and the resources needed to deliver the units into the battle space and then keep the airhead supplied. Such forces, trained to a very high standard and composed of many of the best men an army had at its disposal, were highly valuable assets whose use would ideally be limited to their initial mission, though this was not always the case. The case of the *Fallschirmjäger* in particular showed how overall manpower shortages and frequent military crises meant that German airborne formations were usually committed in an infantry role (albeit an elite one), something that also happened with the 505th PRCT in Italy and both the 82d and 101st Airborne divisions during the Ardennes offensive. Despite reverses such as Arnhem, the efficacy and

A blanket covers a paratrooper killed on the second day of action near Sainte-Mère-Église, Normandy. After the action in the Netherlands the 82d Airborne Division would continue fighting in the Rhineland and the Ardennes, ending the war in the heart of Germany. Throughout the course of the war the division fought during five campaigns in 422 days of combat and suffered 19,586 casualties, including 2,655 men killed in action, and 1,600 more missing in action as of October 1945 (LoFaro 2011: 558). (Bob Landry/The LIFE Picture Collection/Getty Images)

Bringing the 8,800 men of the 82d Airborne Division home to the United States, the *Queen Mary* troopship docks in New York Harbor, colorful banners streaming down her sides. (Bettmann/Getty Images)

value of airborne attack had been proved time and again. It was clear to the senior Wehrmacht officers, discussing the utility of air-landed forces after the war, that "Despite the cost in men and matériel, airborne operations offer such outstanding advantages that no future belligerent with the necessary means at his disposal can be expected to forego using this combat method" (PAM 20-232 1951: 42).

The Wehrmacht's early attempts at fending off airborne incursions were less than successful, partly due to the inexperience of the units involved (as was the case in Sicily) and to the logistical problems that were inherent in any static defensive posture (shown in Normandy), but by the later stages of the war the German Army understood its limitations as well as the vulnerabilities of an air-landed enemy, amply demonstrated in its operations against the Allied airheads during Operation *Market Garden*. Even so, the constant losses of men and matériel coupled with an ever-worsening logistical situation meant that the German ability to defend against Allied air-landing operations was being eroded on an almost daily basis. Barely six months after the battles in the Netherlands, airborne warfare reached its apotheosis with the insertion of 16,000 men in a single day during Operation *Varsity*, an air-landing that

> was supported not only by a large-scale commitment of air forces, totaling more than 8,500 combat planes in addition to over 2,000 transport planes, but also by the entire artillery on the western bank of the Rhine. It was practically a mass crossing of the river by air. The operation was a complete success for it was impossible to take any effective countermeasures. The German troops struck by the attack – worn-out divisions with limited fighting strength – defended their positions for only a short time before they were defeated. (PAM 20-232 1951: 35)

When properly planned and executed, airborne operations were fiendishly difficult to counter effectively, they could deliver tactically critical victories, and they cast a strategic shadow that had the capability to threaten entire theaters of operation.

UNIT ORGANIZATIONS

82d Airborne Division

Although the 82d Airborne Division was initially designated to have one parachute and two glider infantry regiments, the balance was reversed by early 1943. According to the 1942–1944 TO&E (October 15, 1942 with changes up to and including the February 24, 1944 revisions), the 82d Airborne Division was 8,596 men strong. As well as an HQ and HQ company (201 men), it included two parachute infantry regiments. The 504th and 505th Parachute Infantry regiments fought with the division in Sicily; the 504th missed D-Day due to its continuing operations on the Italian front, so it was replaced by the 507th and 508th Parachute Infantry regiments, the 507th being transferred to the 17th Airborne Division after Normandy. The 82d Airborne Division also included the 325th Glider Infantry Regiment (1,608 men, mainly due to having two battalions instead of three like a parachute infantry regiment), including an antitank battery of eight 37mm M3 guns, though by the time of the Normandy invasion most units had adopted the much more effective 57mm M1 antitank gun.

The 82d Airborne Division also fielded an artillery regiment (1,898 men and 36 75mm M1 pack howitzers), comprising two parachute battalions and one glider battalion. Also, even though it was not on the official TO&E until December 1944, the 82d and 101st Airborne divisions managed to add a fourth battalion, equipped with the purpose-built 105mm M3 howitzer, in time for D-Day. Initially the airborne formations had been allocated the lightweight 75mm M1 pack howitzer as their divisional artillery, but the more powerful M3 was becoming available by 1944 (the M1 fired a 14.6lb round 9,600yd, whereas the M3 could fire a 33lb round 8,300yd – a shorter range, but a much more significant impact). Supporting units included an engineer battalion (566 men), a quartermaster company (91 men), a signal company (100 men), an antiaircraft battalion (504 men, 36 .50-caliber M2 heavy machine guns, and 24 37mm M1 antiaircraft guns), an ordnance company (77 men), a medical attachment (305 men), and a military-police platoon (38 men).

A parachute infantry regiment had 2,020 men – 142 officers and 1,878 enlisted – organized into an HQ and HQ company (152 men, including five M1 – later M1A1 – bazookas), three parachute infantry battalions (530 men each), a regimental service company (207 men), and an attached medical/chaplain unit (71 men). A parachute infantry battalion had an HQ and HQ company (149 men including a 42-man machine-gun platoon with eight .30-caliber M1919A4 machine guns, a 39-man mortar platoon with four 81mm M1 mortars, and nine M1 – later M1A1 – bazookas), and three rifle companies (127 men each). A rifle company had an HQ element (19 men including one bazooka) and three rifle platoons (36 men each). Each rifle platoon had an HQ element (six men), two rifle squads (each with 12 men and one or two light machine guns, either M1919A4s or an M1919A4 and an M1928A2 BAR), and a mortar squad (six men with a 60mm M2 mortar).

German formations

On Sicily in 1943, the armored element of Panzer-Division *Hermann Göring* was Panzer-Regiment *Hermann Göring*, which consisted of two *Panzer-Abteilungen* (I. Abteilung with 32 PzKpfw IV and seven Panzerbefehlswagen IV tanks, and II. Abteilung with 43 PzKpfw III and three PzKpfw III Ausf N tanks armed with the short-barreled 7.5cm KwK 37 gun), and one *Sturmgeschütz-Bataillon* (20 StuG and nine StuH assault guns). In addition, a heavy company was attached to the regiment just prior to the invasion, 2./sPzAbt 504, which fielded 17 PzKpfw VI tanks (Jentz 1996). The division was supposed to have two *Panzergrenadier-Regimenter* (Panzergrenadier-Regimenter *Hermann Göring* 1 and 2), each with three rifle battalions, one infantry-gun company, and one antitank company, but at the time of the invasion only three understrength battalions were formed. The division also fielded Panzer-Aufklärungs-Abteilung *Hermann Göring*; FlaK-Regiment *Hermann Göring* (two, later three *Abteilungen*); Panzer-Artillerie-Regiment *Hermann Göring* (three, later four *Abteilungen*); Panzer-Pionier-Bataillon *Hermann Göring*;

Offering a rate of fire of 1,200 rounds per minute, Germany's 7.92mm MG 42 machine gun proved to be a superb weapon that fulfilled the role of squad light machine gun, as well as a heavy machine gun capable of area denial and sustained fire when mounted on a tripod. (NRA Museums, NRAmuseums.com)

and Panzer-Nachrichten-Abteilung *Hermann Göring* (Williamson 2003: 9; D'Este 1989: 604).

91. Luftlande-Division's strength at the start of the Normandy invasion was likely around 7,000–8,000 men. The division consisted of two *Grenadier-Regimenter* (1057 and 1058), each with 2,008 men if they had been at full strength. A *Grenadier-Regiment* had three *Grenadier-Bataillone*, one *Infanteriegeschütz-Kompanie* (infantry-gun company), and one *Panzerjäger-Kompanie* (antitank company). A *Grenadier-Bataillon* was 708 men strong and comprised three *Schützen-Kompanien* (rifle companies) each with three *Züge* (rifle platoons), and one heavy-weapons company (six medium machine guns, three light machine guns, and six 8cm GrW 34 and four 12cm GrW 42 mortars). The divisional guns were in Gebirgs-Artillerie-Regiment 191, which had three *Abteilungen*, each with three *Batterien* (I. and II. Abteilungen, each with 12 10.5cm GebH 40 mountain howitzers, and III. Abteilung with 12 8.8cm PaK 43 antitank guns). The combat-engineer element, Pionier-Bataillon 191, fielded two companies. In place of an *Aufklärungs-Abteilung* (reconnaissance unit), 91. Luftlande-Division had Füsilier-Bataillon 191, which had no headquarters element and was made up of three independent companies: Fahrräd-Kompanie 191 (a bicycle-mounted infantry company),

Panzerjäger-Kompanie 191 (six 7.5cm PaK 40 antitank guns), and FlaK-Kompanie 191 (12 2cm Gebirgsflak 38 antiaircraft guns). In addition, the division had a small contingent of attached armor in the shape of Panzer-Ersatz- und Ausbildungs-Abteilung 100, made up almost entirely from captured French tanks. On June 6 the *Abteilung* had 17 Renault R 35, eight Hotchkiss H 38 or H 39, one Somua S 35, one Char B2, and one PzKpfw III (Murphy 2009: 198–200).

There was a bewildering range of German units fighting in and around Nijmegen in September 1944. Kampfgruppe *Henke* fielded about 750 troops based around elements of Fallschirm-Panzer-Ersatz- und Ausbildungs-Regiment *Hermann Göring*, including its Unteroffiziers-Lehr-Kompanie 29, along with replacement troops from Ersatz-Bataillon 6 from Wehrkreis VI (Zaloga 2014: 48). 10. SS-Panzer-Division *Frundsberg* supplied the forces for Kampfgruppe *Reinhold*, Kampfgruppe *Baumgärtel*, and Kampfgruppe *Euling*. The main elements of the division were SS-Panzergrenadier-Regimenter 21 and 22; SS-Panzer-Regiment 10 *Langemark*; SS-Panzerjäger-Abteilung 10; SS-Sturmgeschütz-Abteilung 10; SS-Panzer-Artillerie-Regiment 10; SS-FlaK-Abteilung 10; SS-Panzer-Aufklärungs-Abteilung 10; and SS-Panzer-Pionier-Bataillon 10.

BIBLIOGRAPHY

82d Airborne Division (1945). *82d Airborne Division in Sicily and Italy*. US Army. Available online at: http://cgsc.cdmhost.com/cdm/singleitem/collection/p4013coll8/id/103/rec/2

Bell, Elmo, (2003). *An Oral History with Brigadier General Elmo Edwin Bell: A Saga of a Survivor*. Hattiesburg, MS: University of Southern Mississippi.

Blair, Clay (1985). *Ridgway's Paratroopers: The American Airborne in World War II*. New York, NY: Doubleday.

Breuer, William B. (1997). *Drop Zone Sicily: Allied Airborne Strike, July 1943*. Novato, CA: Presidio Press.

Burriss, T. Moffatt (2000). *Strike and Hold: A Memoir of the 82nd Airborne in World War II*. Washington, DC: Brassey's.

D'Este, Carlo (1989). *Bitter Victory: The Battle for Sicily, 1943*. Glasgow: Fontana/Collins.

Dolan, John J. (1959). Letter to James M. Gavin, March 15, 1959. Cornelius Ryan Collection, Alden Library, Ohio University. Available online at: http://www.thedropzone.org/europe/Normandy/dolan.html

FM 31-30 (1942). *Tactics and Technique of Air-borne Troops*. Washington, DC: US Government Printing Office.

Fürbringer, Herbert (1984). *9. SS-Panzer-Division. Hohenstaufen 1944: Normandie–Tarnopol–Arnhem*. Saint-Martin-des-Entrées: Heimdal.

Gavin, James M. (1944). *82nd Airborne Division: Operation Market: Historical Data*. Fort Bragg, NC: 82d Airborne Division. Available online at: http://cgsc.cdmhost.com/cdm/singleitem/collection/p4013coll8/id/387/rec/2

Gavin, James M. (1978). *On to Berlin: Battles of an Airborne Commander, 1943–1946*. New York, NY: The Viking Press.

Gavin, James M. (1980). *Airborne Warfare*. Nashville, TN: The Battery Press, Inc.

Gellhorn, Martha (1944). *Rough and Tumble*. Found in: *Collier's Weekly*, December 2, 1944, p. 12. Available online at: http://www.unz.org/Pub/Colliers-1944dec02-00012

General Board Report 16 (1946). *Organization, Equipment and Tactical Employment of the Airborne Division*. General Board, US Forces, European Theater. Available online at: http://cdm16635.contentdm.oclc.org/cdm/compoundobject/collection/p16635coll14/id/36778/rec/1

Henkemans, Nils (2007a). *Panzer Ersatz und Ausbildungs Abteilung 100 in Normandy, Take 2*. Available online at: http://www.network54.com/Forum/47207/thread/1174669606

Henkemans, Nils (2007b). *Panzers on the Cotentin, Take 3*. Available online at: http://www.network54.com/Forum/47207/thread/1192224502

Heydte, Friedrich-August, Freiherr von der (1954). *6th Parachute Regiment (1 May–20 Aug. 1944)*. Manuscript B-839: Historical Division, US Army Europe.

Huston, James A. (1972). *Out of the Blue: US Army Airborne Operations in World War II*. West Lafayette, IN: Purdue University Studies.

Isby, David C., ed. (2004). *The German Army at D-Day: Fighting the Invasion*. London: Greenhill.

Jacobus, George, ed. (1992). *Echoes of the Warriors. Personal experiences of the enlisted men and officers of E Company of the 505th Parachute Infantry Regiment, 82nd Airborne in World War II*. 82nd Airborne Division Association.

Jentz, Thomas L., ed. (1996). *Panzertruppen 2. The Complete Guide to the Creation & Combat Employment of Germany's Tank Force 1943–1945*. Atglen, PA: Schiffer.

Kappel, Carl W. (1947). *The Operations of Company H, 504th Parachute Infantry (82nd Airborne Division) in the Invasion of Holland 17–21 September 1944 (Personal Experience of a Rifle Company Commander)*. Advanced Infantry Officers Course 1948–1949. Fort Benning, GA: Academic Department, The Infantry School.

Kershaw, Robert (2004). *It Never Snows in September: The German View of Market-Garden and the Battle of Arnhem, September 1944*. Horsham: Ian Allan.

Kesselring, Albert (1954). *Kesselring: A Soldier's Record*. New York, NY: William Morrow & Co.

Krafft, Sepp (1944). *Report of the SS Panzer Grenadier Depot and Reserve Battalion 16. The battle at Arnhem 17 Sep 44 - 7 Oct 44*. English translation in AFM File 48, in PRO AIR 20/2333.

Kurowski, Franz, trans. David Johnston (1995). *The History of the Fallschirm Panzerkorps Hermann Göring*. Winnipeg: J.J. Fedorowicz.

LoFaro, Guy (2011). *The Sword of St. Michael: The 82nd Airborne Division in World War II*. Cambridge, MA: Da Capo Press.

Lord, William G. (1948). *History of the 508th Parachute Infantry.* Washington, DC: Infantry Journal Press.

Lunteren, Frank van (2014). *The Battle of the Bridges: The 504th Parachute Infantry Regiment in Operation Market Garden.* Havertown, PA: Casemate.

McQuaid, B.J. (1944). "Nazis Died Like Flies in the Battle of Nijmegen Bridge," in *Los Angeles Times,* October 10, 1944.

Megellas, James (2003). *All the Way to Berlin: A Paratrooper at War in Europe.* New York, NY: Presidio Press.

Michaelis, Rolf (2004). *Die 10. SS-Panzer-Division 'Frundsberg'.* Berlin: Michaelis-Verlag.

Murphy, Robert M. (2009). *No Better Place to Die: Ste-Mère Eglise, June 1944: The Battle for La Fière Bridge.* Havertown, PA: Casemate.

Nordyke, Phil (2008). *More Than Courage: The Combat History of the 504th Parachute Infantry Regiment in World War II.* Minneapolis, MN: Zenith Press.

Nordyke, Phil (2010a). *All American, All the Way: From Sicily to Normandy. A Combat History of the 82nd Airborne Division in World War II.* Minneapolis, MN: Zenith Press.

Nordyke, Phil (2010b). *Four Stars of Valor: The Combat History of the 505th Parachute Infantry Regiment in World War II.* Minneapolis, MN: Zenith Press.

O'Donnell, Patrick K., ed. (2002). *Beyond Valor: World War II's Rangers and Airborne Veterans Reveal the Heart of Combat.* New York, NY: Touchstone.

PAM 20-232 (1951). *Airborne Operations. A German Appraisal.* Washington, DC: Center for Military History. Available online at: https://archive.org/details/PAM20-232

Pegler, Martin (2010). *The Thompson Submachine Gun: From Prohibition Chicago to World War II.* Weapon 1. Oxford: Osprey.

Ridgway, Matthew B & Martin, Harold H. (1956). *Soldier: The Memoirs of Matthew B. Ridgway.* New York, NY: Harper & Bros.

Rottman, Gordon L. (2006a). *US Airborne Units in the Mediterranean Theater 1942–44.* Battle Orders 22. Oxford: Osprey.

Rottman, Gordon L. (2006b). *World War II Airborne Warfare Tactics.* Elite 136. Oxford: Osprey.

Rottman, Gordon L. (2010). *World War II Battlefield Communications.* Elite 181. Oxford: Osprey.

Rottman, Gordon L. (2014). *US World War II Parachute Infantry Regiments.* Elite 198. Oxford: Osprey.

Ruggero, Ed (2003). *Combat Jump: The Young Men Who Led the Assault into Fortress Europe, July 1943.* New York, NY: HarperCollins.

Schlieben, Karl-Wilhelm von (1954). *The German 709th Infantry Division During the Fighting in Normandy.* Manuscript B-845: Historical Division, US Army Europe.

Shilleto, Carl (2001). *Utah Beach, St-Mère-Église: VII Corps, 82nd and 101st Airborne Divisions.* Barnsley: Leo Cooper.

Skeat, C.N.R. (1994). *A study of the Wehrmacht's Ability to Improvise Effective Ad-hoc Battle Groups During Operation Market Garden.* Camberley: Army Staff College.

Smith, Carl (2000). *US Paratrooper 1941–45.* Warrior 26. Oxford: Osprey.

Stenger, Dieter (2017). *Panzers East and West: The German 10th SS Panzer Division from the Eastern Front to Normandy.* Guilford, CT: Stackpole.

Thomas, Nigel (2000). *The German Army 1939–45 (5): Western Front 1943–45.* Men-at-Arms 336. Oxford: Osprey.

Verier, Mike (2001). *82nd Airborne Division 'All American'.* Horsham: Ian Allan.

Westermann, Edward B. (2001). *Flak: German Anti-Aircraft Defenses 1914–1945.* Lawrence, KS: University Press of Kansas.

Williamson, Gordon (2003). *The 'Hermann Göring' Division.* Men-at-Arms 385. Oxford: Osprey.

Wolfe, Martin (1993). *Green Light! A Troop Carrier Squadron's War from Normandy to the Rhine.* Washington, DC: Center for Air Force History.

Zaloga, Steven J. (2004). *D-Day 1944 (2): Utah Beach & the Airborne Landings.* Campaign 104. Oxford: Osprey.

Zaloga, Steven J. (2007). *US Airborne Divisions in the ETO 1944–45.* Battle Orders 25. Oxford: Osprey.

Zaloga, Steven J. (2013). *Sicily 1943: The Debut of Allied Joint Operations.* Campaign 251. Oxford: Osprey.

Zaloga, Steven J. (2014). *Operation Market-Garden 1944 (1): The American Airborne Missions.* Campaign 270. Oxford: Osprey.

Zetterling, Niklas (2000). *Normandy 1944: German Military Organization, Combat Power and Organizational Effectiveness.* Winnipeg: J.J. Fedorowicz.

INDEX

References to illustrations are shown in **bold**.